Hope in Pastoral Care
and Counseling

**Also by Andrew D. Lester
from Westminster John Knox Press**

When Children Suffer: A Sourcebook
for Ministry with Children in Crisis (Ed.)

Pastoral Care with Children in Crisis

Coping with Your Anger: A Christian Guide

Hope in Pastoral Care and Counseling

Andrew D. Lester

Westminster John Knox Press
LOUISVILLE
LONDON · LEIDEN

Scripture quotations from the New Revised Standard Version of the Bible are copyright © 1989 by the Division of Christian Education of the National Council of the Churches of Christ in the U.S.A. and are used by permission.

Book design by Drew Stevens
Cover design by Tanya R. Hahn

First edition

Published by Westminster John Knox Press
Louisville, Kentucky

This book is printed on acid-free paper that meets the American National Standards Institute Z39.48 standard. ⊗

PRINTED IN THE UNITED STATES OF AMERICA

01 02 03 04 — 10 9 8 7 6 5 4

Library of Congress Cataloging-in-Publication Data

Lester, Andrew D., date.
    Hope in pastoral care and counseling / Andrew D. Lester. — 1st ed.
      p.   cm.
    Includes bibliographical references and index.
    ISBN 0-664-25588-4 (alk. paper)
    1. Pastoral counseling. 2. Hope. 3. Hope—Case studies.
  4. Despair. 5. Despair—Case studies.   I. Title.
  BV4012.2.L47   1995
  253.5—dc20   94-36895

Contents

Acknowledgments

My gratitude is expressed to Dean Leo Perdue and the faculty of Brite Divinity School for providing me with a Summer Research Stipend and to Dean Perdue and William Koehler, Provost of Texas Christian University, for granting me a paid leave of absence. Their support allowed the concentrated time so crucial to completing such a project. Numerous members of M.Div. classes and Ph.D. seminars, plus participants in continuing education events and professional conferences, have contributed both experientially and conceptually to this project. My thanks also to clients and students who have willingly offered their personal experiences as clinical material.

Friends and colleagues have invigorated me through conversation and graciously critiqued various portions of early drafts. Their comments identified weak links in the presentation and enabled me to strengthen the manuscript. My gratitude is expressed to Alan Culpepper, Doug Dickens, Larry Easterling, Bryan Feille, Dave Gouwens, Stan Hagadone, Dick Hester, James Hyde, Steve Ivy, Jane Johnson, Ann Letson, Wayne Oates, Nancy Ramsay, Ann Redmond, and Cheryl and Ron Sisk.

Stephanie Egnotovich, managing editor at Westminster John Knox Press, was encouraging and insightful throughout the process. Harold Twiss offered invaluable editorial guidance. Sharlie Tomlinson generously offered secretarial assistance, which freed my time and energy and protected me from many mistakes. Dawn Darwin cheerfully persevered in the task of tracking down resources, references, and editorial changes. Margaret Wintersole provided creative commentary on style and grammar.

For more than a decade I have attempted to wrap my mind and heart around the subject of hope—a difficult and challenging process. Many friends and colleagues have put up with my incessant conversation about the subject and my expressions of frustration about the process, but none more than Judy, my wife of thirty-four wonderful years. This book is dedicated to her in gratitude for her faithful nurture, steadfast support, and unwavering faith that the project was worthwhile.

Introduction

> Hope is fundamental to human life. Indeed if we are to continue as individuals and as a species it is something we require as much as bread and water. Yet in the main, hope is a neglected topic, especially among scholars.
>
> —Ross Fitzgerald, *The Sources of Hope*

A significant responsibility and privilege of ministry is to nurture hope and confront despair. Pastoral care and counseling are historically concerned with healing, guiding, sustaining, reconciling, and liberating.[1] When people are wounded and in need of healing, confused and in need of guidance, overwhelmed and in need of sustaining, alienated and in need of reconciliation, or trapped and in need of liberation, it should be obvious that hope and despair are major psychological and theological dynamics.

Some years ago Wayne Oates and I edited original clinical pastoral research that focused on persons who were struggling with crises that came with hemodialysis, physical disability, the birth of mentally challenged children, the diagnosis of cancer in a child, and so forth. We found that the authors had drawn similar conclusions when making suggestions for the practice of pastoral care and counseling. They called attention to the struggle with the breakdown brought about by these crises of what I will call in this book "future stories." These persons were worried not about their past or even their present suffering, but about what would happen in the future. Despair was the major threat, and hope was the central psychological and theological issue with which they were struggling. Hope, or its absence in despair, is the basic psychospiritual dynamic with which the pastoral caregiver must contend, particularly when attending to a crisis. As Oates and I summarized,

> Lastly, we call attention to the overarching and undergirding theme of the book—*hope*. The pastor represents hope to persons who face the unalterable, the unknown, or the frightening.... In an age when despair,

discouragement, and disillusionment are the predominant emotional dynamics, it becomes increasingly necessary for the Christian faith to unmask, refurbish, and communicate its belief in hope.[2]

Since despair is so painful and debilitating, and because hope is so basic to living joyfully, I am convinced that we need to be more explicit about our commitment to a God who is out in front of us calling us into an open-ended future. The Judeo-Christian tradition has always been teleological, believing that creation is going somewhere and proclaiming a future for humankind that transcends the obvious. Pastoral caregivers represent a God who is aligned "against the forces of futurelessness."[3] Despair can be seen as an enemy, and pastoral caregivers bring their knowledge and skills into combat against it. Indeed we represent to our parishioners (as pastors), clients (as pastoral counselors), or patients (as chaplains) a hope based on the promises of God that a new future is always available to us, that numerous possibilities exist in every present circumstance.

The Neglect of Hope

Pastoral theology is concerned with developing theological perspectives that inform all pastoral functions, but it is particularly interested in providing a theological frame of reference for pastoral care and counseling ministries. A primary task of pastoral theology is to develop the theological lens through which we as practitioners of pastoral care and counseling can understand the human condition and organize an effective pastoral response.

Nearly two decades ago, Robert Carrigan challenged pastoral theologians and pastoral counselors by pointing out the vital role that hope plays in pastoral care. As he observed,

> in the face of all this new attention given to hope by theologians, philosophers, psychotherapists, and psychologists, it seems strange that there has been little or no attention given to the phenomenon of hope by pastoral theologians and counselors.[4]

He was referring to the work of the "theologians of hope"[5] who were then publishing important works on the future dimensions of faith and the centrality of hope and eschatology for Christian theology.

Regrettably, this theology of hope has had little impact on the literature in pastoral care and counseling. Given the suffering that is routinely faced by pastors, chaplains, and pastoral counselors as they minister to people who are drowning in despair, Carrigan was amazed that "there has been no reflective writing on hope or model of hope in pastoral psychology." He then asked, "Why is it that those of us in pastoral theology are not dealing with so important a topic?"[6]

I think the primary answer to Carrigan's question has to do with the failure of pastoral theology to develop a theological anthropology (an understanding of the human condition) that provides an adequate frame of reference for addressing the subject of hope. John Macquarrie said, "It has been my contention for a long time that the doctrine of [persons] is the right starting point for a contemporary theology."[7] Intense study of human beings by both the physical and social sciences has changed the nature of philosophical and theological inquiry about humanity.

Wolfhart Pannenberg argues that "Christian theology in the modern age must provide itself with a foundation in general anthropological studies."[8] He points out that understanding human interaction with the world, both the physical and cultural environment, is now the foundation for theological reflection. Theological anthropology today should not start with dogmatic presuppositions about humankind, but rather turn

> its attention directly to the phenomena of human existence as investigated in human biology, psychology, cultural anthropology, or sociology and [examine] the findings of these disciplines with an eye to implications that may be relevant to religion and theology.[9]

Modern theologians, including pastoral theologians, to be credible, must now begin their enterprise with an anthropological foundation for understanding religious experience. In our day any explanation or defense of the faith must be fought "on the terrain of the interpretation of human existence."[10]

For two decades pastoral care and counseling has been appropriately critiqued for its dependence on "the images and concepts, the presuppositions and ontological assumptions of the psychological and behavioral sciences."[11] One central piece of the ontological assumptions of these disciplines is anthropology. A basic reason we have neglected the subject of hope is that pastoral care and counseling is taught and practiced on the basis of perceptions about the nature of human existence rooted in the anthropological worldviews of the social and behavioral sciences.[12]

The social and behavioral sciences have made significant contributions to anthropology, of course, and no theology of personhood can be credible that does not attend to the insights provided by these disciplines. We are enriched by the psychoanalytic worldview that has led us to appreciate the influence of the past on human personality. We have also learned more about the significance of present circumstances on any person's life situation from social learning theories, cognitive theories, systems theories, and marriage and family therapy.

The fact that humans are constantly moving into the future dimension of temporality, however, has been neglected. The anthropological assumptions that inform psychological theories and therapies have overlooked the future dimension of human consciousness of time. The past and present are foundational, of course, and we have learned many helpful concepts about the contributions of these two time dimensions to the human predicament. I will argue, however, that equal time for the future dimension is necessary for a more holistic psychological and theological understanding of what Anton Boisen called "the living human document." [13] The phrase "human document" is Boisen's way of reminding us that any human being is a unique text that must be read (heard) and interpreted (the hermeneutical task).

Because pastoral care and counseling march primarily to the social science drummers, our theory and practice also are hindered by an anthropology that does not include a fully developed view of time-consciousness. Pastoral theology, consequently, has ignored a significant aspect of the human condition, namely our temporality—the fact that we are constantly embedded in the context of time, which includes both past *and future*. By neglecting the future aspects of time-consciousness, pastoral theology has not fulfilled its mission of providing a theological lens through which pastoral care and counseling can develop creative methodologies for nurturing hope and combating despair. Construction of a viable pastoral theology of hope is impossible without developing theories about the significance of future dimensions of time-consciousness in human existence.

Pastoral theology at its best allows mutual critique between knowledge generated by the human sciences on the one hand and the wisdom of the Christian tradition found in biblical, historical, ethical, philosophical, and systematic theology on the other. Ideally, this discipline integrates what seems truthful from both into a holistic, anthropologically sound theology. Pastoral theology must attend to the anthropological concepts of time as conceptualized by philosophy, the human sciences, and systematic theology. Furthermore, we must reexamine the relationship of time-consciousness to the experience of suffering. Out of this dialogue can be constructed a pastoral theology of hope.

A paradigm shift for pastoral care and counseling is under way.[14] Pastoral theologians and pastoral care specialists have been taking a fresh look at the contributions that theological paradigms offer to our understandings of the human condition. I want to expand the basic paradigm that informs how we think about what Boisen called the "human document." More specifically, I want to change the lens through which we understand what causes people to lose touch with hope and fall into the abyss of despair. This book adds the dimensions of existential future and theological hope to the categories of thought used by pastoral caregivers. This expanded paradigm should affect both our theoretical assessments and our clinical interventions.

Preview

Following Pannenberg's suggestion, my first three chapters will establish an anthropological context in which to root a pastoral theology of hope. I will identify and describe three sources for this theological anthropology. The first source is the concept of *temporality*, the recognition that human beings experience their consciousness of time in three tenses: past, present, and future. Chapter 1 gleans from several existentialist philosophers and theologians the idea that temporality is a basic context for human consciousness. Furthermore, though recognizing the interconnectedness of all three dimensions of time and appreciating the contributions of past and present to personal identity, I will establish the significance of our capacity to anticipate the future for understanding human experience with hope and despair. I will point out that the social and behavioral sciences, particularly psychological theories and therapies, have not understood the significance of the future dimension of temporality.

The second source is *narrative theory*, which establishes that selfhood is created in story form. Chapter 2 demonstrates that selfhood is formed through narrative structuring, a process rooted in and inclusive of all three dimensions of temporality. Narrative has become a respected metaphor for conceptualizing the meaning-making nature of human beings, the process of making sense out of life's ongoing events. Narrative theorists have demonstrated that a person's sense of self develops out of the stories through which he or she interprets experience. These stories collect both the remembered past and the imagined future, which are then integrated into the person's present identity, another contribution to understanding temporality.

A person's sense of identity is certainly formed by personal history, captured in stories about the past, and it is being continuously understood by the stories we are shaping in the present. My focus, however, will be on the process by which humans project themselves into the future and the reality that these future stories are an important contributor to a person's core narratives. A narrative cannot exist without a plot. Stories must answer the question, Where is all this going? A person's core narratives are composed of stories about the future as well as about the past and present. Projecting ourselves into the future and creating stories about the "not yet" is a central process of any person's ongoing identity, the self in process. The content of these future stories is both a contributor to and an expression of a person's hoping process. Future stories, of course, are also the source of despair.

The third source is a *phenomenological assessment of human brokenness*. I will demonstrate that wounds to the human spirit are created not only by the personal history that lies behind us and the present circumstances that surround us but also by changed perceptions of the future that is approaching. Chapter 3 shows how human brokenness and suffering are related not only to past experiences and present circumstances but also to problems in our future stories and the hoping process.

Although all humans have a future tense, they experience the future from a variety of perspectives, depending on their unique mixture of cognitive and affective responses to past and present experiences. For some the future is a blessing; for others it seems like a curse, depending on the character of their future stories. One sad consequence of our neglect of the future tense is that we fail to attend to one of the most significant themes and dynamics of vital religious experience—*hope*—and one of the most oppressive aspects of cognitive, affective, and spiritual suffering—*despair.*

The relationship between future dimensions of time-consciousness and hope is explored in chapter 4. After describing hope, I discuss the hoping process and how it attaches to both finite hopes and transfinite hope. I demonstrate that though hope is rooted in personal history and affected by present circumstances, it is energized from the projected perceptions of the future that lie in the anticipatory consciousness of each individual.

Chapter 5 offers a description of despair that ties this existential experience to the same ontological realities as hope. Like hope, despair is tied to future stories. When future stories are lost or distorted, then we are vulnerable to despair. Future stories can become dysfunctional, meaning they no longer contribute to hope but lead rather to despair.

In chapter 6 I explore the differences between hope and despair in relation to three themes: reality, possibility, and community. Understanding the conflicting dynamics of hope and despair will provide guidance for pastoral care and counseling processes that facilitate restructuring future stories that are hopeful.

The pastoral theology of hope developed in chapters 1 through 6 provides an expanded paradigm for the practice of pastoral care and counseling. The theoretical material suggests significant changes in methodology at all levels of pastoral caregiving—crisis intervention, supportive pastoral care, short-term pastoral counseling, and/or more extensive pastoral psychotherapy. The final four chapters discuss and illustrate clinical strategies that enable people to recover hope.

Exploration of future stories, obviously, is the place to start. To understand what people are experiencing in their present situation, particularly related to a breakdown in the hoping process, we must find out what they are perceiving about the future. We must know what they are anticipating, whether consciously or unconsciously, in order to understand their despair. Pastoral caregivers have been carefully trained to uncover and evaluate past and present stories, but we have few guidelines for discovering and assessing future stories. To assess accurately a human problem and to offer effective pastoral care and counseling demands skill in exploring a person's future stories. Chapter 7 discusses practical strategies for discerning the future dimension through pastoral conversation.

Some people find it difficult to talk about the future. People suppress future stories just as they suppress past events, so some future stories are unconscious. Chapter 8 examines some of the reasons for resistance to the exploration of future dimensions of time-conconsciousness. Some future stories are dreadful and create so much anxiety that the person would rather not share them because of the resultant pain that surfaces. Other future stories would be embarrassing if they were made public, so the fear of ridicule or rejection keeps them secret. "Magical thinking," the fear of making something come true by stating it in words, also keeps people wary of sharing future stories.

When we explore future stories with a person who is experiencing hopelessness, we will find that her or his most dominant future stories are dysfunctional—future stories that do not contribute to hope but instead make the person vulnerable to despair. Chapter 9 describes how to help people deconstruct dysfunctional future stories, a first step in making room for the construction of creative future stories. "Deconstruction" is a concept I borrow from literary criticism and psychotherapy. It describes a process by which a narrative (whether a written text or a lived text) is assessed and critiqued.

Chapter 10 outlines strategies for reframing and constructing hopeful future stories. Revisioning attends to the future dimensions of a person's sacred story, which contributes to healing dysfunctional future stories and hoping processes.

Pastoral theologians struggle to integrate the classical theological disciplines with the human sciences while placing both in the crucible of pastoral practice. My dual identity as a professor and a practitioner pushes me toward integration of theology and ministry. Both my pedagogical commitments and practical experience suggest that theory building and clinical ministry are integrally related and must be held in the tension of mutual nourishment and critique. I am hoping that both academicians and clinicians will profit from this endeavor.

The theoretical ideas in this work have been developed and then challenged in the context of my interactions with clients, patients, supervisees, and students. Conversely, my theoretical explorations provided new shapes to my understanding of the "human document," which creatively modified the methodology of my practice. In summary, the development of these ideas, both theoretical and methodological, has occurred in an interactive process. Presenting them here as they developed chronologically would be difficult, so I have succumbed to tradition and presented them in summary fashion.

Although the theoretical material is necessarily streamlined, I hope that it will nonetheless expand paradigms for both academicians and clinicians. I hope the clinical material will challenge pastoral theologians and pastoral caregivers to reexamine both the scope and effectiveness of ministry practice and whet their appetites for building additional models of hope and despair.

Case material comes primarily from my work as a pastoral counselor but also from pastoral care experiences in the local church, in the hospital, and in supervising residents in training programs accredited by the Association for Clinical Pastoral Education and the American Association of Pastoral Counselors. Clinical material has been read and corroborated by the individuals on whom it is based and published with their permission, except for brief vignettes that are unidentifiable. Verbatim material was transcribed from tape or reconstructed after the interview. Names, of course, are fictitious, and some data have been deleted or changed to protect confidentiality.

I trust you will interact with this material out of your own personal and professional pilgrimage and consider publishing your unique insights on this subject. Testing these ideas in the clinical ministry of pastoral care and counseling will enable you to critique the theory and contribute to the further development of these ideas. We need to create a body of literature on pastoral theological understandings of hope (clinical case material, theoretical concepts, and personal experience) that will inform our ministry and the ministry of those who follow.

Perhaps later research will reveal gender differences in time-consciousness and the hoping process. I have intentionally used inclusive language, and brackets within quotations from copyrighted material indicate editing that has been done to make the language inclusive.

Part 1

Pastoral Theology and Hope

1

The Power of Future
in Human Existence

The primary phenomenon of primordial and authentic temporality
is the future.

—Martin Heidegger, *Being and Time*

If the salvation in the gospel is to become flesh . . . it is not enough
that something is above us. There must be that which is before us.

—Ernst Bloch, *The Principle of Hope*

Calendars, datebooks, flight schedules, and alarm clocks exist only to
remind us that another deadline approaches. Time is passing, we say,
and the future is coming at us. All cultures take note of the progression
of days and nights, the cycle of growing seasons, and the process of
aging. Time-consciousness is a phenomenon that calls for interpretation, an awareness that must be imbued with some meaning.[1] As Stephen Crites has written,

> the fact that there are very different notions of time implicit in the cul-
> tural forms of different historical traditions does not contradict the inher-
> ent temporality of all possible experience. . . . It is impossible that a
> culture could offer no interpretation of this temporality at all.[2]

Philosophers, theologians, and psychologists all confront time-
consciousness when trying to interpret human experience.[3] Novelists
and playwrights must use the flow of time to convey story and drama.

This chapter addresses five areas. It (1) establishes that our awareness of time is basic to the existential context in which human consciousness functions, (2) emphasizes the crucial role played by the
future dimension of this time-consciousness in identity formation and
the process of living, (3) describes the neglect of future time-
consciousness in personality theory and psychotherapeutic methodologies, (4) summarizes how temporality and future tense are two central
concepts from philosophical anthropology that contribute to a pastoral
theology of hope, and (5) describes some specific areas of pastoral care
and counseling practice affected by these ideas.

Time and Existence

Existential philosophers remind us that at any *present* moment you and I are affected both by a *past* that we can remember and interpret and by a *future* that we can anticipate and invest with meaning. Existentialists call this basic characteristic of the human condition our *temporality*.[4] Existentialists will not let us forget that both past and future dimensions of time-consciousness are foundational elements within our experience of "self-in-the-world," the here and now of living.

Exploring Temporality

Augustine explores the concept of time with curiosity and wonder in his *Confessions*.[5] His understanding of temporality begins with the logical certainty that only the present moment really exists. He explores the paradoxical fact that although the past is gone and the future has not arrived (hence neither actually exists), both are existentially real. Because he understood that both past and future are conscious modes of temporality necessary to our very existence and our understanding of being, he knew that the present cannot be the only time frame that actually exists. Augustine solves this paradox by claiming that our present moments include our conscious awareness of past and future.

Augustine identifies *memory* as the aspect of consciousness that makes the past available in the present. The foresight of *expectation* is the aspect of conscious awareness that brings the possibilities of the future into the present. Consciousness links the three tenses of human awareness through memory and anticipation into a unified sense of self. Augustine summarizes this as "the present of things past is memory, the present of things present is direct attention, the present of things future is anticipation."[6]

John Macquarrie ties Augustine's categories to existential concepts of temporality, saying that through memory, persons bring their past into the present, and by "anticipation and imagination" they already possess a future and project themselves into it.[7] In Macquarrie's words, "Through memory, we bring with us our past; through anticipation and the projects of the will, we reach out into our future."[8] Crites, a modern philosopher of religion, also demonstrates that Augustine's insights continue to be relevant for our understanding of temporality. Crites is convinced that "our sense of personal identity depends upon the continuity of experience through time, a continuity bridging even the cleft between remembered past and projected future."[9] This continuity of experience is maintained because our conscious awareness of the present moment is a process that always works between the past remembered and the future projected. Elaborating on Augustine's categories, Crites says of the present moment, "memory is its depth [and] anticipation is its trajectory."[10] He believes that the present tense is able to create a unified life experience by mediating the tension between the past, which is fixed and cannot be undone (although it can be reinterpreted), and the future, which is "still fluid [and] subject to alternative scenarios."[11]

Søren Kierkegaard's conceptualization of human existence includes a temporal framework that depends on a balance of past, present, and future dimensions of time-consciousness for structuring personality. The authentic self, according to Kierkegaard, is an entity with three fundamental components: *necessity, freedom*, and *possibility*. The authentic self exists by maintaining a relationship among these three dimensions of existence, which are closely related to past, present, and future.[12]

Necessity, or the "actuality" as Kierkegaard also called it, is that dimension of selfhood that is rooted in three realities of our existence. First, we are completely dependent on God for our existence. Second, the specifics of our personhood such as genetic makeup, physical appearance, mental abilities, family of origin, and environment are givens. Third, some aspects of our personhood result from choices we have exercised in the past and thus now make up part of our identity. These three realities constitute what we might call the real self. Kierkegaard connects the necessity aspect of the self with what already exists, with the past that cannot be changed.[13]

Although we are always conditioned by these necessary aspects of the self, we are never totally bound by them. For Kierkegaard, the lives of human beings are not predetermined; people are free to pursue possibilities in life. Possibility has to do with the potential for change and development, or as Kierkegaard indicates, in order to become a self, we must reflect through the medium of imagination the infinite possibilities coming into view.[14] Through imagination humans can pursue these possibilities and construct a future that is different from the past. He believes that possibilities are somewhat limited by the actualities but that the future is open-ended. In Kierkegaard's thought, though the actualities of life condition a person, humans also possess the freedom to act within the limits of necessity.[15]

For Kierkegaard, then, individuals are conditioned and limited by their past, yet free to seek possibilities in the future. This freedom is found in the present, which provides us with the opportunity to move beyond the actualities of our self in order to develop our potential. The core aspect of the self is the freedom component, the dynamic center that keeps necessity and possibility in equilibrium. In Kierkegaard's theology this freedom is part of God's intended creation, an innate characteristic of our existence.

Living as an authentic self, for Kierkegaard, means taking seriously more than our immediate necessities. We must also anticipate the future with the awareness that we have the freedom to actualize our potential and the responsibility to give shape to this future. Being authentic includes being realistic about the past, expectant about the future, actively engaged in the present, and as a result—hopeful.

Existentialism and Temporality

If we are to understand the human experience of temporality, we must think of time as a totality, a unity of consciousness that includes past and future. Existentialists wrestle with the rational awareness that each moment of the present is but an instant between past and future. Every here-and-now experience (whether cognition, perception, choice, behavior, or emotion) is significantly affected by both the past and future dimensions of time. Past, present, and future are for the human mind and heart the "three dimensions or directions into which the human sense of time extends and which in their togetherness constitute the present moment."[16]

Our consciousness of time is not the record of a series of events that are noticed separately, as if they were individual occurrences unrelated to or isolated from each other. Rather, time is the way in which we organize the succession of single events into a whole that makes sense. Both cognitive perceptions of time and intuited experiences of time join in providing us with a sense of continuity between past and future that allows us to place ourselves in the flow of time.[17] Our conscious self organizes past, present, and future into a holistic perspective that constitutes the temporal context for shaping our identity.

We are aware that objects and things, like rocks or houses, have a past (they have been existing before this moment), a present (they are existing right now), and a future (they will in all probability exist tomorrow). Objects, however, are neither self-transcendent nor conscious of time, both of which are basic distinguishing marks of the human species, from the existentialist perspective. Therefore, the facts of the past and future of objects are irrelevant to their present moment. But for humans, what has gone before and what is anticipated are relevant to the present moment. The capacity for self-transcendent consciousness allows us to remember the events of the past and to anticipate that the future is coming, both of which affect the way we live in the present.

Conscious awareness of future tense comes early in life. A young child's ability to anticipate a change of diaper or the arrival of food in response to a cry is an early sign of expectation. When a child plays peekaboo, the expectation of seeing the parent's face again generates the sense of excitement. The development of memory about what *has* happened gives the basic content for projection and the awareness that something *can* happen. Watching a child's anticipation as she plays with a toy to accomplish a certain result, such as pushing a button to make a noise or pulling a lever to make something jump, reminds us how quickly the future tense becomes available to us. The mental capacity of children to be self-conscious about the future dimension of temporality develops rather quickly.[18] They easily learn that something is going to happen or could happen that is not happening now. Herein lie the origins of our mental capacity for hope.

Existentialists also use the word *temporality* to describe our embeddedness in time, the fact that we are creatures who are at every moment of our existence both bound by and potentially freed by time. To be bound by time means that we cannot escape the passing of time, the insistent march of our future through the present moment into our past. We can neither stop the process of time nor return to and change what is past (although we can change our interpretations of the past).

Time is also a source of human freedom. Time provides the stage on which we give shape to our selfhood, our community—indeed, to the future of humankind. Because we are self-conscious creatures, aware of both the past that is gone and the future that is coming, time provides the possibility of development, change, healing, and liberation. As Ernst Bloch put it, "[Hope is] bursting open our present, connecting us with our past, and driving us toward the horizons of the not-yet-realized future."[19] I now turn to a discussion of how our opportunity to dream, to plan, to control, and to decide stretches into the future dimension of our consciousness.

The Significance of Future Tense

I have already stressed the essential unity and connectedness of past, present, and future dimensions in the overall time-consciousness of human beings. Since we are focused on the place of hope in human existence, however, we must explore the significant role that future tense plays in human existence. We will find that hope, although rooted in the past and acted out in the present, receives its energy from the future. Paul Tillich has observed that to understand the present means to see it in its inner tension toward the future … finding amid all the infinite aspirations and tensions which every present contains not only those which conserve the past but also those which are creatively new and pregnant with the future.[20]

Before exploring Tillich's concepts further, I want to illustrate the importance of knowing past, present, *and future* dimensions of a person's life for making sense out of any human situation.

A Dramatic Illustration

Playwright Terrence McNally in his play *Lips Together, Teeth Apart*[21] provides an insightful example of our multi-tensed existence. This drama illustrates how important temporality, particularly the future tense, is to understanding the human condition. McNally tells the story of two couples (John and Chloe, Sam and Sally) who spend the fourth of July together at a beach cottage. Sam, the husband of Sally, and Chloe, the wife of John, are also brother and sister.

The *present tense* of the play reveals the cryptic tension among all four characters. The playwright creatively communicates the pain that so frequently exists in close relationships. The interactions of the characters reveal various personality traits and lifestyles that make it difficult for each character to relate intimately with the others.

As the play progresses, McNally demonstrates his awareness of the influence of personal history by revealing the *past tense* of both the individual characters and the familial relationships that give shape to the tension. Sam admits that he has felt ridiculed and rejected since childhood and suspects that people talk about him behind his back. Sally's brother, from whom she inherited the beach cottage, was gay and died of AIDS. John bemoans his loss of an overprotected but happy childhood. Sam reveals that he suffers from anxiety attacks expressed through the inability to tie his tie and extreme difficulty in swallowing. John and Sally have had a sexual encounter, a fact that Sam can't confirm and Chloe won't face. From these pieces of information the audience appreciates McNally's insight about how past experience sets the stage for the present interactions.

Central for our discussion, however, is the masterful way McNally demonstrates that these characters and their interactions can be fully understood only as the *future tense* of their situation is revealed. As the play unfolds, McNally frequently suspends scenes, darkens the stage, and has the characters privately unveil their expectations about the future to the audience. By withholding the information about future projections from the other characters, McNally demonstrates how the characters misunderstand their spouses and friends because they are aware of only past and present data (take note, pastoral caregivers). They do not possess the empathic understanding that knowledge of a person's future projections can provide.

Sally reveals that she is pregnant and shares with the audience her fear of either having another miscarriage or watching her child grow up gay. Sam sheds light on his anxiety attacks when he tells us that he is terrified of becoming a father and feels certain that he would be totally inadequate. He also describes to the audience his fear of being abandoned by Sally and his anxiety about what he would do without her. John's future tense is dominated by the fact that he is dying of esophageal cancer. Hearing this frightening future projection, the audience suddenly has a new understanding of John's threatened masculinity and Chloe's overly solicitous behavior toward him. Her hyperactivity and manic functioning, which provide much of the play's humor, immediately make sense in light of her own anticipatory grief—her future projection about the loss of her husband.

As each future story is revealed, members of the audience begin to think, "Oh, of course, now it makes sense!" The play makes abundantly clear that we cannot understand the emotional tone or the behavior of these characters if we do not know the future they perceive to be bearing down on them. Although their past and present stories are foundational and determinative, the unfolding revelation of the future tense makes the selfhood of each character intelligible and energizes the play.

The Future and Becoming

As noted, the existentialists insist on the continuity of past, present, and future in the human experience of time. They generally agree, however, that future tense is more unique in defining the human condition. Martin Heidegger, for example, claimed that "the primary meaning of existentiality is the future." [22] When discussing time, he "always mentioned the future first . . . to indicate that the future has a priority in . . . authentic temporality." [23]

As members of the animal world, we are motivated by survival and we function accordingly. Being conscious of future time, however, allows us to give meaning to our existence so that we construct purposes for survival that create future goals. Being self-transcendent, we decide whether life is meaningful or meaningless. To fully comprehend human beings is impossible without understanding what purposes pull us into the future and what meanings we attach to these purposes.

Existentialists give priority to future tense when exploring the uniqueness of personal identity-in-the-making. They are forceful and eloquent when discussing the influence of future time on the unique melody of an individual's life. For Jean-Paul Sartre, for example, future tense provides the most important clues to a person's identity. Only we humans have "potentiality" as part of our basic nature. This potentiality, by which Sartre meant the capacity for "becoming," is based on knowledge of the past but depends for actualization on conscious awareness of the future in which becoming occurs. The present tense of anyone's existence, he argued, would have no meaning at all were it not for the future possibilities inherent in her or his existence. In Sartre's words, "The Future is the continual possibilization of possibles— as the meaning of the present." [24] Existentialists frequently emphasize the effect of future possibilities on human self-consciousness.

Existential theories about temporality and the primacy of the future tense influence therapeutic practice. Existentialist psychotherapists share with psychoanalytically oriented practitioners an awareness of the effect of past experience on a person's sense of self-in-the-world. However, they are more interested in future projections. Irvin Yalom, a contemporary existentialist psychotherapist, points out that exploring the "deep" does not necessarily mean exploring the past. From his perspective the most profound concerns that a patient can experience are the ultimate concerns that are rooted in the past but are primarily related to future projections. As he says,

> The past—that is, one's memory of the past—is important insofar as it is part of one's current existence and has contributed to one's current mode of facing one's ultimate concerns; but it is . . . not the most rewarding area for therapeutic exploration. The future-becoming-present is the primary tense of existential therapy.[25]

In summary, the future tense grants to the present tense the gift of possibility. The self-who-is-becoming, the self who is exploring possibility, is the primary modality for authentic selfhood. Future stories, as well as past and present stories, are essential in defining a person and in making that person's being-in-the-world intelligible.

The Philosophy of Possibility

Philosopher Ernst Bloch has developed a whole system of thought around the future tense of human temporality. Known as "the philosopher of hope," Bloch created an ontology based on possibility (not-yet-being) and an anthropology centered on human beings as hopers (not-yet-conscious). In *The Principle of Hope*, Bloch argues that "openness toward the future," both in the cosmos and in human consciousness, is the basic principle out of which reality emerges.[26]

At the age of twenty-two, Bloch developed the concept of *anticipatory consciousness* that became the cornerstone of his life's work.[27] He believed that the human capacity to hope, which grows out of anticipatory consciousness, is the core ingredient of human existence. For Bloch, the existence of this phenomenon is the major piece of evidence that proves the open-ended nature of reality. He thought the existence of hope made the future more open, undetermined, and filled with possibilities than philosophers understood.

Bloch called for a new understanding of the basic ontological structure that shapes the nature of reality. "I contend," he said, "that the world is open, that objectively real possibility exists in it, and not simply determined necessity or mechanical determinism."[28] The nature of reality is not already in "being," but lies ahead in an open-ended future, what Bloch called the "not-yet-being." Ontological structures are open to an undetermined and as-yet-unimaginable future that will unfold as the not-yet moves toward us.

What led Bloch to these conclusions? His philosophy of hope, both ontological and anthropological, was conceived not in the context of theism but from a phenomenological perspective. He was amazed that humans have the capacity to imagine and project beyond what can be experienced or accomplished in their present circumstances. He considered human expectation and anticipation as ontological data that should be taken seriously by philosophers as they construct worldviews. Much of Bloch's *The Principle of Hope* is a description of the various utopian ways humans have desired more than can be realized in their present world. This phenomenological observation became the focal point of Bloch's philosophy.

Self-Awareness of Future Tense

Attending to how our daily existence reflects involvement in all three time dimensions is a personal way of increasing awareness of our temporality and particularly the dominance of the future tense. The significance of the past-tense dimension of temporality is obvious. The discipline called history uncovers, organizes, and interprets our past. The media frequently refer to things that happened in times past. In private thinking and interpersonal conversations we refer to stories about personal, family, and cultural history. We may discuss how our identity has been shaped by our family of origin, our early object relations, and our communal/cultural environment.

The present often appears to be the dominant dimension of our temporality. We are conscious, perhaps overly aware, of our present situation—what is happening today in our family, workplace, relationships, church, politics, and professional organizations. The here-and-now decisions, functions, and deadlines—what we are doing right now—seem so prominent and consume such focus of attention that the significance of the future-tense dimension of temporality to our present life may not be obvious.

We can easily underestimate the amount of time and energy we spend thinking about and working toward the future dimension of our lives. This evening I reviewed my activities for the day just to see how many of them had to do primarily with my future. I was surprised at the result. The telephone calls alone were more future-oriented than I would have imagined. I had two conversations with my insurance agent concerning policy consolidations that would change my premium payments in six years; I talked with a committee chairperson about a workshop presentation for a convention next year, and I spent an hour on the phone planning a trip overseas that was eight months away. Furthermore, I attended a committee planning meeting for a degree program that will not start for two years, and I worked on this manuscript, which will not be published for more than a year.

In short, my present-tense day was spent in large part anticipating and planning for my future. Anticipation of future events gave specific meaning to my present functioning and explained why I expended my time and energy as I did. You could not understand me or my behavior without attending to my future anticipations. I would have to agree with Kurt Reinhardt that

> the future . . . is not something wholly indefinite that will occur at some later date and therefore does not concern me at this present moment. The future is already alive in human hopes and fears, in human planning and designing: it is a formative force and an integral part of the present.[29]

Think about the amount of time and energy you give to your own future agenda, projecting into the not-yet, giving shape to possibilities, and developing future stories. How much time do you spend planning for trips and engagements in the future? Or thinking about where your aging parents will live if their ability to take care of themselves declines? Or discussing the future of your favorite sports team: drafts, signings, schedules, and play-offs? How much time goes into planning for your vocational future: new programs, staff additions, personnel changes, promotions, and continuing education? And what amount of your time is spent on your financial future, as you study and keep up with pension plans, social security concerns, and investments? Once we begin to measure how much psychic energy is expended on future expectations or concerns, it becomes more difficult to frame personality and day-to-day existence as if they were primarily shaped by our past and present.

Personality Theories and
Psychotherapeutic Practice
Overlook Future Tense

As psychology separated from its roots in philosophy and theology, it tended to neglect time-consciousness as an aspect of the human condition that merited reflection and research. Depth psychology and existentialism have their roots in the same culture, but psychology has not paid much attention to the existential issue of temporality, particularly the future tense. Generally speaking, the continuity of past, present, and future in human consciousness, is missing from the philosophical anthropology that underlies most behavioral and social science theories of personality. More specifically, the future tense is frequently dismissed as unknown or unpredictable at best, and full of illusion, fantasy, and religious ideation at worst.

Psychoanalytic models, for example, build theories of personality structure on how one copes with basic sexual and aggressive instincts or on what happens (or doesn't happen) in a person's earliest relationships with significant others. The discovery of the unconscious, of course, was a major development in psychological anthropology that has immeasurably increased our knowledge of personality, specifically how the past affects the development of selfhood—the characterological structure, personality traits, and behavioral patterns in the present. Understandably, psychoanalytic theory and therapy focus attention on the past dimensions of human temporality.

Social learning models of personality (such as cognitive theories, systems theories, and marriage and family therapy), while appreciating that past experience shapes personality, still emphasize the present environment. When assessing or explaining a person's present thoughts, feelings, and behaviors, social learning theories usually focus on current life situations. These theories have made significant contributions to our understanding of marital and family dynamics, cognitive sets, and the influence of current interpersonal relationships and environmental context. The impact of the future dimension of human temporality on our identity, our behavior, and our problems, is largely ignored.

Furthermore, when personality theory is based on understanding the past and/or present, then the therapeutic models generated by these theories will follow suit, primarily focusing on the past and/or present. Therapeutic processes, which build on psychoanalytic models, are primarily focused on changing lives by exploring and uncovering the past. The goal is to help people gain insight that can facilitate new decisions about living in the present. Most psychotherapeutic strategy based on these models does not acknowledge how much our present situation is shaped by what Bloch called our anticipatory consciousness, our projections into the future.

Social learning models of therapy focus on changing the present dynamics in a person's belief system or in the structures, functions, and behaviors of the interpersonal systems in which he or she lives and works. Past and present tense are normatively the only dimensions of time subject to psychotherapeutic interventions. The future dimension of human existence is frequently unattended in the therapeutic process.

Because the future dimension of temporality is neglected, the subject of hope is also ignored in the behavioral and social sciences literature. Psychiatrist Robert Beavers and psychologist Florence Kaslow are aware that hope is "a crucial dimension in therapy" and express concern about the lack of research and writing on hope in their disciplines. They point out that "the cultivation of hope and the abolition of despair are prime ingredients in psychotherapy, yet have received little attention in the therapeutic literature." [30]

Toward a Pastoral Theology

Pastoral theology must begin its study of hope and despair on the anthropological cornerstone of human temporality. Our first building block is time-consciousness as a foundational ingredient of the existential context in which we live. Human beings are multi-tensed, which does not refer to being stressed in numerous ways but means rather that we have a past tense, a present tense, and a future tense. Authentic existence includes accepting the givens imposed by time past, living with the freedoms provided in the present, and shaping the possibilities that the future presents.

Traditionally, when Christian thinkers have interpreted Paul's trilogy of faith, hope, and love to dimensions of time-consciousness, they have often related faith to the past, love to the present, and hope to the future. This is a mistake, however, for all three spiritual dynamics have their place in, and connection with, each time dimension. Hope is rooted in the past because we remember the mighty acts of God and our personal encounters with the transcendent. Hope is empowered from the future from where it receives its vision. Finally, hope is active in the present as it energizes and motivates us to live so that God's "will be done on earth as it is in heaven."

Theology views time not only in the historical sense of past, present, and future but also in relation to the activity of God. In christological formulations we express that past promises and future fulfillment have somehow come together in the person of Jesus the Christ. God acted in a present moment of real time (the Christ event), which now lies in the past but has changed the course of human possibility. Our future is open in a new way because of the advent of the Christ. The realm of God was activated in the past and is here in the present, yet its completion is out in front of us in the not-yet.

The second anthropological building block for a pastoral theological study of hope can be stated as follows: Within the context of temporality the future dimension of time-consciousness makes a unique contribution to the human enterprise. Hope is primarily attached to our conscious and unconscious projection toward, expectation of, and investment in the future-tense dimension of conscious awareness. Therefore, anthropological views that primarily emphasize the past- and present-tense experience of human existence do not lend themselves to a thorough exploration of the dynamics of hope—or to its absence, in despair. Future is the dimension of finitude that is less fixed, the dimension of time that provides the potential for growth, development, and becoming. Within our future projections exist the content and the end-settings of our purposes and meanings. The future is the predominant home of hope and despair.

Pastoral theology embraces the theological anthropology developed by the "eschatological theologians." Heavily influenced by Bloch, the central figure in this movement, Jürgen Moltmann calls attention to the importance of the future dimension of time-consciousness. He argues that human beings learn of their basic nature not from their present perceptions of selfhood but from the future. Humans are grounded in history, a history that is "open to the future, open for new, promised possibilities of being."[31] Moltmann takes the stance that the basic identity of a person is hidden and can be revealed only by those unseen possibilities that lie beyond the future horizon. Basic to the nature of human beings is their being "always on the way towards some . . . expected future whole." This future is the stage on which a person "can become what [one] is not yet."[32]

A pastoral theology of hope, then, must emphasize that from both philosophical and theological-anthropological perspectives, temporality, particularly the capacity to anticipate the future and to project ourselves into this future, is part of our very being.

A theological statement about creation must include temporality as both a mark of our finitude and as a gift that sets parameters for our identity as creatures. Consciousness of time keeps us grounded, yet within the boundaries of finitude, provides us with the freedom to become. Our future orientation, the gift of seeking, searching, desiring, expecting, is a necessary context for responding to the God who loves us. The ability to respond to and seek relationship with the Creator makes sense only in the context of temporality, specifically the open-endedness of our future orientation.

Pastoral Care and Counseling:
Theory and Practice

These first two building blocks of pastoral anthropology lead to some obvious conclusions for both the theory and practice of pastoral care and counseling. First, comprehending human existence holistically is not possible unless we understand a particular person from the perspective of all three time dimensions. To understand ourselves fully is to remember our temporality, that in our present moment we are surrounded by time past and time future. Pastoral care and counseling with people infected with hopelessness involves helping them evaluate their stance toward each dimension of time.

We have established that historically the behavioral and social sciences have been most proficient at understanding human beings by analyzing and assessing the past and/or present dimensions of their existence. Theoretical and methodological approaches to pastoral care and counseling have been significantly informed and influenced by psychoanalytic and social learning perspectives on personality theory and therapy. Our knowledge of the influence of past history and present circumstances helps us immeasurably in our understanding of personality development, intrapsychic dynamics, interpersonal relationships, the cultural environment, and other factors that shape human beings. Pastoral care specialists have developed expertise in using these insights about personal history and present situations in facilitating the healing process. As important as it is, however, this knowledge about the human condition must be expanded to include future perspectives.

The human sciences have neglected the future-tense dimension of human existence both in developing personality theories and in their methodological strategies, whether assessment procedures or therapeutic strategies. Pastoral care and counseling, under the influence of the behavioral and social scientists, has also left the future tense unattended in formulations about the human condition. The influence of future projections on our present actions, thoughts, and feelings has been underestimated. Human beings are shaped and influenced by these images of the not-yet as well as by what happened in their past and is happening in their present. Pastoral care specialists must make sure that their own theory and practice are based on a more complete theological anthropology.

I am not asking you here to give up your present personality theory or method of therapy, whether it be one of the psychodynamic models or one of the systems theories. This is not an attempt to discount or discredit the personality theories and therapeutic modalities in which you were trained and with which you feel the most comfortable. Nor do I attempt to change your use of these theories as a lens for understanding the human condition.

If your orientation is psychodynamic and you believe that the human condition is primarily shaped by events that have occurred in the past and driven by interior mechanisms and psychic processes inherent to our biological existence, then I would confirm the importance of the insights gained. However, these mechanisms and processes work within the framework of temporality and in the context of a person's entire experience of time-consciousness. This means that a person's mental processes have occurred within the context of future tense as it was perceived at any given time and have also affected future tense as imagined at any given time. The person (or family or group) before you in the present moment was shaped by perceptions of the future coming at that person at every point in her or his history. At any point in a person's past, he or she was also projecting into the future.

The same is true if your orientation is related to social learning theories and you believe that the human predicament is primarily molded (1) by the current marital, familial, communal, and cultural systems in which they are immersed or (2) by the belief systems to which they adhere. These systems all operate in the context of time-consciousness, having both a remembered past and an anticipated future. Any system is affected by both the past stories and the future stories that give shape to the system. Cognitive sets, frames of reference, and constructions of reality all embrace and are inclusive of future-tense projections. People do not develop perceptions of reality or interpret the world around them without input from each time dimension, particularly from the future tense.

This book will demonstrate that to the degree we embrace a personality theory and therapeutic methodology that does not take the future dimension of human temporality seriously, to that degree is our personality theory and methodology (though helpful in many ways) incomplete and inadequate. In other words, if the anthropological concepts that underlie our understanding of personality and therapeutic methodology fail to recognize that individuals and groups are embedded in total time-consciousness, then our anthropological assumptions cannot provide an adequate theological context for the unique commitments and tasks of pastoral care and counseling: healing, sustaining, guiding, reconciling, and liberating.

Pastoral assessment, for example, must include exploration of a person's future projections. The theological anthropology established here makes clear that we cannot fully comprehend a present situation or crisis unless we know the role of the future tense. As we shall discuss in a later chapter, hearing the whole story of a person's life situation must include gathering information about future perceptions, not just past and present experiences.

Pastoral intervention is also enlightened. When involved in any pastoral care event we must remember that the stressful situation is happening within the context of a time frame that includes both a history and expectations. All the people involved are being influenced by both their past history and their future projections. To give effective and creative care we must attend to what we will call in the next chapter *future stories*.

We must ask how human beings incorporate and make sense out of their multi-tensed existence, particularly the future tense and its possibilities. For the answer we turn in chapter 2 to narrative theory.

2
Narrative Theory and Future Stories

This is what fools people: humans are always tellers of tales, we live surrounded by our stories and the stories of others, we see everything that happens to us through these stories; and we try to live our lives as if we were telling a story.

—Jean-Paul Sartre

Social scientists are rediscovering the unity of body/mind/spirit that characterizes the human being. Frustrated with reductionist concepts that blur the distinctions between human beings and machines, both theorists and therapists have been developing new paradigms for addressing the more profound philosophical and psychological questions about human existence. *Narrative theory* is making a major contribution. Theodore Sarbin, a theoretical psychologist, suggests that the concept of "narrative" has gained the right to function as a new "root metaphor" for "the task of interpreting and explaining" the human condition.[1] Narrative psychology is providing fresh ways of framing the human situation.[2]

Narrative theory, furthermore, is contributing significantly to theoretical developments in religious studies. Scholars are using narrative concepts as tools for interpreting the biblical material.[3] Narrative theology offers new perspectives for understanding religious experience.[4] Narrative theory can make an important contribution to the philosophical and theological anthropology that supports a pastoral theology of hope.

A Narrative Understanding
of Human Existence

Narrative theory proposes that "narrative structure" is a meaningful organizing principle for understanding human behavior. Organizing principles are guiding metaphors, whether mechanistic or humanistic, that explain how "human beings impose structure on the flow of experience."[5] The "narratory principle," as Sarbin calls it, posits "that human beings think, perceive, imagine, and make moral choices according to narrative structures."[6]

Stephen Crites was one of the first to conceptualize that human life occurs in narrative form. In a landmark article in 1971, he wrote that "the formal quality of experience through time is inherently narrative."[7] As we humans encounter the world, we organize and make sense out of our experience by means of narration. Each new sensation, stimulus, and interpersonal transaction is shaped by our mental processes into a story.

The natural and automatic process of narrative structuring constantly organizes our perceptions, though we pay little attention to this process. An example occurred last night when I heard a wild pack of dogs barking ferociously in the woods behind our house. My mind asked, What's happening? I remembered the doe grazing there several days earlier and immediately formed a story: the dogs were either on her trail or already had her trapped. Because I did not think she could survive a pack of dogs, my story left me grieved. Another example is what happens when the telephone rings late at night. As we reach to answer it, we imagine several possible explanations, all in fragmented story form.

Stanley Hauerwas, another proponent of the narrative perspective, establishes that knowing the whole narrative is basic to our knowledge of a situation because "it is only through narrative that we can catch the connections between actions."[8] As I jog past a three-year-old girl, I hear her ask her mother, "Where is he going?" In trying to make sense out of the jogging action the young girl calls for a story that interprets and thereby provides understanding and meaning. "The most essential ingredient of narrative accounting (or storytelling)," Mary and Kenneth Gergen wrote, "is its capability to structure events in such a way that they demonstrate, first, a connectedness or coherence, and second, a sense of movement or direction through time."[9] Humans usually experience action and behavior as organized by time, which necessitates the construction of stories that provide comprehension.

The young girl wanted an explanation for the jogging, but she needed an answer that captured a time frame. Where is this action going? What happens next? What is the plot? The answers, of course, form a story. As the Gergens point out, stories provide "directionality," because making sense out of an event necessitates understanding its process.[10] An event accrues meaning only as we apply narrative structure that connects the event to its impact on the future—the consequences for the rest of the story.

The whole context of a narrative includes all three dimensions of our temporality. Each dimension is integrated into the full narrative structure out of which a person is operating at any given moment. This narrative, of course, includes the unique confluence of past experience and future anticipations at that particular point in the flow of a person's life.

Narrative theorists build an anthropology that stresses both the unity and the context of human experience. They demonstrate how theories that attempt to study one specific aspect (event, role, function) of human life fail to appreciate the essential unity of the human self. They agree that we cannot grasp fully the reality of human experience unless each particular behavior is "understandable and intelligible." [11] They argue, however, that making human behavior intelligible results not from isolating aspects of human behavior for study but in comprehending the whole context in which a particular behavior is embedded. [12] Events make sense only if we can use what Jerome Bruner called the "narrative mode" to explain the purposes of human intention which are organized within time. [13]

This context can be known only if we know the full narrative history of the individual, because actions flow "intelligibly from a human agent's intentions, motives, passions and purposes." [14] Hauerwas puts it this way:

> A story, thus, is a narrative account that binds events and agents together in an intelligible pattern. . . . there is no other way we can articulate the richness of intentional activity—that is, behavior that is purposeful but not necessary. [15]

To know a person's full narrative, therefore, including its forward thrust, is imperative when trying to make sense of any person's life situation.

Narrative and Identity

Narrative theory provides an alternative way of comprehending selfhood and personal identity. Research in narrative theory, both in psychology and theology, has confirmed that human personality is storied. [16] Human beings do not simply tell stories, or illustrate their lives with storytelling. We construct our sense of identity out of stories, both conscious stories and those we suppress.

Research in child development demonstrates that children register their experiences prior to verbalization, so in that sense our personal narratives begin at least by birth. [17] When we get old enough we assign words to our various experiences. Language, Crites said, "is a necessary mark of being human, i.e., being capable of having a history." [18] We use our newfound language to describe and interpret life events in the shape of stories that include our future anticipations.

Not all that happens in our environment is captured. We are selective about our response to all the stimuli that occur continuously in our environment. Those to which we attend become the experiences that we incorporate into our stories.[19] Given the uniqueness of our physical, characterological, and experiential history, each of us interprets a stimulus differently. The Gergens contend that a basic task of narrative structuring is to establish connectedness and coherence within a person's identity, which enables a person to make sense out of life.[20] As we move through life, new experiences are not only integrated into the developing core narratives but also bring change into these core narratives.

In this book I define a *core narrative* as the central interpretive theme that provides an individual or system with an overarching structure (composed of numerous smaller stories) that organizes and makes sense out of a particular aspect of the human condition. Individuals have core narratives that structure their understandings and values around concepts such as marriage, money, sex, discipline, work, and so forth. Within a person's religious faith will be core narratives that explain such concepts as suffering, church, and prayer.

Our experiences, then, are given their individual distinctiveness, their form as *our* story, through the structure of narrative.[21] Our sense of self, our identity, is built piece by piece as we form our experiences into stories and then integrate these stories into our ongoing core narratives. As we shall see later, a breakdown in core narratives makes one vulnerable to despair.

The core narratives of a person's life, rather than mere data about them, set the parameters of that individual's sense of self. Simply referring to facts about a person does not really allow us to know that person. We cannot effectively answer the question, *Who is she?* says Hannah Arendt, by describing the *what* about her (such as a description of physical attributes, facts about vocation, or information about organizational memberships) because in presenting such lists of characteristics the person's uniqueness escapes us.[22] The question, Who is she? can be answered only by referring to the whole "story" of that individual. We do not sense that we really know someone until we begin to hear that person's story and identify the core narratives. The core narratives communicate a person's values, purposes, and unique characteristics, which allow us to imagine an identity. Indeed, we begin to form our own story about that person. Narrative is the structure by which we construct our experiences of others as well as of ourselves. Revealing our stories, likewise, is the only effective way to communicate our sense of self to another person.

Narrative and Social
Construction Theory

Narrative theory has many connections to social construction theory. Scholars of all disciplines have been interested for centuries in the philosophical questions about *what* we know (the nature of reality) and *how* we come to know what we know (the epistemological question). In Western culture we have assumed that an objective reality exists, and our theories and perceptions can accurately reflect it. In this century, however, researchers are increasingly aware that reality is not as objective as imagined. One theory that responds to this awareness is constructivism.

Constructivist theory posits that the ideas we have about the world are not exact replicas, not pictures or maps of the "real" world, but instead are constructs, or perceptions of the world which we build in our minds as we encounter the world.[23] Reality for each of us is actually our subjective interpretation of our experience with external things, social structures, and relational happenings. Constructivist theory, which evolved not only from psychological research but from research in the hard sciences,[24] has demonstrated that even the sensory data that we "take in" is selected by physiological (particularly neurological) givens.[25] From a constructivist perspective the narratives that make up our worldview reflect only our unique interpretations of the world and are not to be confused with the real world. In this sense each person must be responsible for her or his feelings, thoughts, and actions in response to the world as she or he perceives it and as these are included in one's core narratives.

Some proponents of this theory, of course, have decided that no reality exists outside of our perceptions, a radical constructivist position. Even so, holding to the existence of an objective world while still recognizing the truths of constructivist theory is quite possible.[26] My purpose here is not to debate the philosophical question, Is there an absolute truth? Constructionist concepts do not have to be tied to that question. Even persons who believe in external truths that transcend human knowledge have difficulty denying that the way individuals shape perceptions of these objective truths is significantly affected by the uniqueness of their experience with the environment and the cultural context in which this experience takes place. Bebe Speed, for example, has described a position that takes both objective reality and subjective construction seriously. His perception of this connection between the constructing knower and the reality that must be known is called "co-constructivism."[27]

How do we construct our unique interpretations and meanings about the world we encounter? Most social construction theorists believe that language is the key. Since we must describe and interpret our experience through communication, language is the central process through which reality is constructed. This concept fits well with narrative theory, which establishes that the process of narrative structuring enables us to make sense of the world. We turn various pieces of sensory data into the form of story in order to grasp its meaning. We bestow meaning upon the sensory data through the narratory principle.

Narrative and Temporality

Narrative theory contributes to our understanding of temporality. Perhaps the most thorough study of the strong connection between narrative and time-consciousness was made by philosopher Paul Ricoeur. He acknowledges the foundational importance of this connection when he says,

> What is ultimately at stake in the case of the structural identity of the narrative function as well as in that of the truth claim of every narrative work, is the temporal character of human experience. The world unfolded by every narrative work is always a temporal world.[28]

Human activity is always temporal, so human consciousness is a continuous stream of responses to the world around us.

Like other thinkers in both philosophy and psychology, Stephen Crites has asked how the present moment can embrace and absorb both past and future. After all, remembering the past and projecting the future are vastly different processes of our self-conscious being-in-the-world. How can these separate modalities of time, remembered past and anticipated future, be joined together by the self? Crites believes this integration is accomplished by the narrative quality of human existence.[29] Or as Ricoeur says, "time becomes human time to the extent it is organized after the manner of narrative; narrative in turn is meaningful to the extent it portrays the features of temporal existence."[30]

Theodore Sarbin refers to the temporal dimension of narrative when he defines story as "a symbolized account of actions of human beings that has a temporal dimension."[31] Stories must take seriously the time frame in which any action, event, or relationship takes place. Crites, too, connects the process of narrative structuring with our awareness of time.[32] This conscious processing of experience into stories, which Kenneth Gergen and Mary Gergen call "self-narratives,"[33] gives continuity to the temporal nature of these events. We connect acts and behaviors into stories that are inclusive of what has gone before, what is happening now, and what we anticipate will happen in the future. Good stories include all three dimensions of time by having a beginning, a middle, and an end,[34] another way of saying past, present, and future.

The structure of a person's identity includes all three dimensions of time-consciousness. The concept of narrative structuring is necessary to explain how human beings establish and integrate their identity, since a sense of self must constantly balance past experience with future expectations. A person's sense of self does not consist only of past stories, those aspects of one's experienced history which make up the conscious continuity of identity and of present stories one is in process of constructing. Selfhood is also formed by future stories, those aspects of one's sense of self which grow out of projections into the future. Thus, the core narratives that form our personal identity are shaped by future anticipations as well as by previous experience.

Narrative theory, therefore, supports the significance of future tense in human existence and contributes to the philosophical anthropology that is foundational to a pastoral theology of hope.

Narrative and Past Tense

Narrative theory, like psychoanalytic theories, gives thoughtful attention to the past. This emphasis on personal history is necessary given the fact that past stories are so foundational for our sense of self. The self "comes into existence only to the extent that it can be recollected out of the past," Crites says.[35] A self-perception does not spring out of nowhere, but has roots in a person's history. Today I listened to a young man say "agnostic is the best way to describe me" and to a thirty-two-year-old woman who continuously used the words "insecure" and "fearful" as she discussed herself. Obviously, past stories contribute to the core narratives that produced these phrases.

What gives our "self" a sense of continuity that allows us to claim it as "me"? Our storied history, created by memories, provides us with the sense of groundedness necessary for having an integrated self. Memory gives us access to past occurrences that are collected and organized into a narrative. A "story-like narrative," Crites said,

> establishes a particularly strong sense of personal continuity, because it can link an indefinite number of remembered episodes from the single point of view of the one who recounts or merely recalls the story. This single point of view is the 'I' who now speaks or recalls, and this 'I' which situates my story and distinguishes it from others also anchors what I call my self in its identity over time.[36]

From our memories develops a life story that provides the context for a sense of personal identity in the present.

To become a self one must appropriate the past. In therapy this integration is usually accomplished through the "archeological dig," an insight-oriented process that enables a client to gather up his or her stories, both conscious and unconscious, and either discover or construct an intelligible narrative that accurately defines the client's personal history and clarifies her or his identity. Clinical experience confirms the assumptions of narrative theory that normally the more complete the story, the more integrated the self.[37]

On the downside, the person who cannot "re-collect" a self out of the past is a psychologically disabled self whose personal boundaries are difficult to establish and who is thus vulnerable to many mental health problems. Many past stories are unconscious because of repression or suppression, which cause difficulties in self-differentiation. Survivors of sexual abuse, for example, have often suppressed past memories because of the dreadful nature of these stories. Associated past stories ("I am a bad person or this would not have happened") are inaccurate self-assessments and create distortions in the survivor's core narrative and, therefore, in her or his identity. Therapy includes both the recovery of unconscious stories and the healing of distorted past stories.

Narrative and Present Tense

The present tense is central in narrative theory because our present moment provides the angle of vision for "re-collecting" the past and shaping it into a coherent whole. The present is the point from which an "I" is remembering, assessing, and organizing a history. This essential process of establishing and claiming a personal identity both influences, and is influenced by, core narratives.

On the one hand, the interpretation of any present experience is significantly affected by the existing narrative. A person's core narratives, which serve as guiding life maps, influence how a new experience is interpreted. In this sense a person's past story is lived out in the "now." Since the present is our only window into the past, insight into a person's past serves as a vehicle for understanding how that person perceives and makes stories out of present occurrences.

Likewise, what happens in the present moments of our lives can affect how we "re-collect" our past experiences. In fact, the "I" who narrates our story about the "me" who is the central figure in the narrative may at any time restructure the narrative on the basis of a current experience. New information can lead to a new frame of reference and a reinterpretation of past events.

Margaret, for example, learned when she was thirty-four years old that her husband was gay. She came to a pastoral counselor because the experience had been so traumatic for her and their three teenage children. During the therapeutic process she had to reshape a number of her past stories on the basis of this new information. She had different interpretations of the dynamics of their sexual relationship, the intensity and intimacy of his friendship with several males, and the disappearance of money over the years. Past stories were now reassessed within a different framework to account for her new knowledge.[38]

The foregoing discussion makes obvious the contribution of past and present stories to our core narratives. In the context of human temporality, however, we must recognize that the core narratives of both our individual and corporate identities include images and expectations about the future.

Narrative Theory and Future Tense

Narrative theorists often say that stories are going somewhere. The continuity of our human dramas reaches beyond the present moment. Any good story begs the hearer to answer the question, What happens next?[39] In this sense a story always assumes future tense and anticipates the next event. Because human beings are "future tensed," we imagine answers to this what-happens-next question by projecting our core narratives into the future.

Crites stresses that a person's life narrative includes the future tense. After establishing that the present moment is the place from which a person's past is "re-collected," assessed, and organized into a sense of identity, he emphasizes that this present moment is not a static point but a process that is "always leaning into that vast unknown that we call the future."[40] He describes the future tense as a "scenario of anticipation,"[41] inclusive of the hunches, guesses, and predictions that shape our images of the future bearing down upon us.

Our self-transcending consciousness gives shape to our past experiences, integrates them with our present context, and allows us to project ourselves into the future by developing scenarios about what is to come. These projections are structured into stories about our future which join with past and present stories to create a unified narrative that is inclusive of all three dimensions of our temporal existence.

From what we experienced in the past and now experience in the present, Crites says, we "pro-ject" images of what our existence will look like in the future. By "framing little stories" about what might happen next, we "orient ourselves to the future." [42] We fill up our future with created content, developing individual and communal stories about the future. These *future stories* make a significant contribution to the fabric of our core narratives, the tapestry from which our ultimate identity is woven. We not only are a self, we are becoming a self, and we give shape to the not-yet-conscious self through the future stories we create.

At any given moment, each of us is working on our self-in-progress, not only by re-assimilating the past and integrating it with the present, but also by using the unique self-transcendent process of imagining our "self" in the future. Our identity, obviously, is not only influenced by the past that we "re-collect" but also by the future that we "pro-ject." We cannot separate "who we have been" and "who we are now" from "who we imagine we are becoming."

To take an event or a behavior out of the flow of time—that is, to separate it from what has already happened, on the one hand, or what one expects to happen, on the other—makes that action unintelligible. Since one purpose of a self-narrative, say the Gergens, is to connect stories into a whole that crosses "temporal boundaries," then isolating an event from its temporal context separates it from the plot and leaves that event without meaning.[43] The meaning we assign to life, or have the potential of assigning, must come from that part of our narrative which reaches into the future. When persons have difficulty connecting their past and future with present experience into coherent narratives, they are seriously impaired. Suicidal ideation can emerge out of a circumstance in which a person's narrative does not make sense as projected into the future and, therefore, no future action makes sense. Any person suffering from any level of despair has failed to form a narrative that effectively connects the present with the past and the future.

To claim that future stories are a significant part of a person's narrative is to recognize that a defining characteristic of narrative is that it is teleological. Like any plot, a person's life narrative has a next scene. "There is no present," Alasdair MacIntyre wrote,

> which is not informed by some image of the future which always presents itself in the form of *telos*—or a variety of ends or goals—towards which we are either moving or failing to move in the present. . . . our lives have a certain form which projects itself towards our future.[44]

The Gergens say this narrative structuring that accounts for human movement through time is accomplished through two related components in stories. First, a narrative must "establish a goal state," by which they mean a valued ending.[45] An individual's biography is going somewhere; it is aimed at something; it has a future reference. We must find out what goal or ending is possible in a person's future story. As individuals and in relationships with others, we all live, as MacIntyre said,

> in the light of certain conceptions of a possible shared future, a future in which certain possibilities beckon us forward and others repel us, some seem already foreclosed and others perhaps inevitable.[46]

The second necessary component in a story, according to the Gergens, is that it must "select and arrange events in such a way that the goal state is rendered more or less probable," meaning it must have a plot that confronts the possibilities that exist in the future.[47] To comprehend a person's core narratives we must understand how those core narratives are imagined and projected into future stories. If the goal is valued and the story contains a plot that makes reaching the goal a possibility, then the future story contributes to hope. If the plot predicts that reaching the valued goal is not possible, then a person is vulnerable to despair.

Community Stories:
The Social Context of Narrative

We know that any individual's narrative is embedded in other narratives. Theologian John Navone says that "life stories interpenetrate" and describes how much of our story develops through appropriating the stories lived out by others. In fact, "The story of a self cannot be told without the stories of other selves."[48] In this sense every individual story is both limited by and explained in some ways by the larger narratives in which that individual's stories have taken shape. "Although self-narratives are possessed by individuals," Kenneth and Mary Gergen wrote, "their genesis and sustenance may be viewed as fundamentally social."[49]

Social construction theory places major emphasis on the contribution of social interaction to an individual's construction of reality.[50] Social constructivists believe people's ideas about life are "socially constructed, communicated and legitimated" within our cultural context.[51]

Each person is constantly evolving a set of meanings and understandings (constructs) about life that reflect what is taught by the individuals and institutions in that person's environment. The family of origin bombards the child with their worldview. As the child's experience widens, so does the barrage of interpretations and belief systems from every corner of the culture. By this socialization process we acquire our frames of reference and create our stories about reality. Personal constructs (perceptions of reality) not only grow out of our encounters with the world but also develop out of our interactions with other persons about these encounters. The specific interpretations and resulting narratives persons impose on any event are influenced by whatever dominating analogies or interpretive frameworks are present in their environment.[52]

A systems perspective offers an angle of vision on this cultural embeddedness. Systems theorists teach us about the influence of our relational environment on our life process, particularly our frames of reference and worldview.[53] Systems develop their own unique narratives. Each family system, for example, has interpreted its past experiences in stories that provide the family with its unique identity. Every family system has core narratives that serve as the lens through which family members interpret present occurrences and relationships. From our earliest caregivers through extended family, teachers, peers, and the media (our communal context)—all have their own stories about the world, which contribute significantly to the narratives that we as individuals develop. "Narratives are preeminently communal products," the Gergens wrote. "They are not the possession of single individuals, but are the byproducts of social interchange."[54]

Individual members will understand the core narratives from a different perspective, depending on their unique experiences of the family. My theoretical and clinical certainty about this truth was confirmed by personal experience with my own siblings. I am the oldest of six, with eighteen years separating me and my brother, the youngest. Several years ago the six of us spent four days talking about growing up together. I was amazed at the unique perspectives on the core narratives of our family, depending on gender, age, birth order, and specific experiences.

Family narratives, of course, develop in the environment of the wider narratives provided by the extended family and the community, which are in turn shaped by still broader narratives that exist in the school system, the geographical region, the socioeconomic group, and the religious tradition to which they belong. The narrative process of any individual (including the language, images, and symbols) is affected by the narrative structuring of the larger culture and the meanings that are attached to life by gender, politics, and ethnic heritage. Sallie McFague describes this process: "We learn who we are through the stories we embrace as our own—the story of my life is structured by the larger stories (social, political, mythic) in which I understand my personal story to take place."[55]

Systems, like individuals, are temporal—having a past, a present, and a future. Families and cultural systems establish their identities not only by the stories that "re-collect" and make meaning out of their past experiences but also by those that project their corporate identity into the future tense. Family, community, and cultural narratives include both implicit and explicit future stories that contribute to the future stories of the individuals in the system. Systems establish future stories that model scenarios that are the "right" ones, the future stories toward which "smart" people, or "good" people, or "Christian" people should be living.

In our day of mass media and pluralistic experience, pastoral caregivers experience both the internal and interpersonal conflict that results as people try to juggle multiple narratives. Often the individuals, couples, and families who seek pastoral intervention are faced with conflicting narrative perspectives on both mundane stories and ultimate belief systems, within the narratives of their larger communities. One man whom I am counseling, for example, is wrestling with images and meanings assigned to human existence by a traditional male-dominated family of origin on the one hand and feminist understandings of egalitarianism encouraged by the educational curriculum of his faith group on the other hand.

Narrative Theology
and Sacred Stories

Since all human life is storied, we must give shape to our religious experience through narrative structuring. As we encounter the numinous in what James Loder calls the "transforming moment" and "convictional experience," [56] we form stories in order to make sense of these experiences. These become our sacred stories, the core narratives that conceptualize and communicate our response to divine/human encounters. I was reminded at a Christmas Eve service of the centrality of our faith stories. The entire service was composed of reading the birth narratives from scripture and singing the hymns that recount and celebrate this event. These narratives not only include stories about the past events, of course, but also stories about future expectations, focused on what the Christ child will mean to the future of humanity.

Each individual has created sacred stories that express personalized understandings of religious faith. These stories will have developed into core narratives that attempt to systematize the content of these stories into religious beliefs. For those with a religious identity, these faith stories make meaning out of religious experiences in the past and also form stories about what they expect in the future.

Christian narrative affirms the centrality of future tense in its understanding of the sacred story. Christian narrative collects and connects the past history of God's actions from creation to incarnation and from exodus to resurrection. The mighty acts of God serve as the guarantee of God's promises for the future. As George Stroup put it,

> The identity of Christian individuals and communities is finally rooted in and dependent on the yet unfinished narrative . . . on the expectation of a future in which God's promises in the past will be consummated in new and unexpected ways.[57]

The sacred story conveys that the community of believers is "on the way," in philosopher Gabriel Marcel's words, and affirms that our narrative reaches into an open-ended future.

Toward a Pastoral Theology

Narrative theory offers another anthropological building block to a pastoral theology of hope. Narrative theory takes human temporality seriously. When people construct their reality, their understanding of the world in which they live, they are conscious of time past, time present, and time future. Although it places appropriate emphasis on past and present dimensions of time-consciousness, narrative theory stresses that all core narratives focus significant energy on the future. The narrative metaphor for understanding human beings contributes to our emphasis on the primacy of future tense for a pastoral theology of hope.

We have established that narrative theory is a paradigm that facilitates our understanding of how selfhood comes into being. We have demonstrated that we project our "selves" into the future, creating future stories that guide our journey into tomorrow and play an important role in our core narratives. Significant energy is expended in directing life toward, or away from, these future stories.

Narrative theory explains that our identity is not only grounded in stories past that affect stories present; stories future also make a significant contribution to that identity. Our consciousness of time makes it necessary to have stories of our past which structure the core narratives *from* which we live, as well as enabling us to create future stories that establish the core narratives *toward* which we live.

Narrative theology specifically describes how we form religious experience into stories of faith. Every sacred story includes not only a past but a future story that empowers life in the present. From a narrative perspective, the sacred story is about the God-who-is-love. How do we know the identity of this God? We must remember that in the same way we answer the who-are-you question about a human person by finding out her or his narrative, so the question, Who is God? must also be answered by knowing the narrative. As Hauerwas says, "God is a particular agent that can be known only as we know [God's] story."[58] Where is this story found? Hauerwas points out that we know God's story through the stories of those who have relationship with God. In scripture, the tradition, and within the community of faith we have the stories of creation and redemption, exodus and deliverance, crucifixion and resurrection. For the Christian, of course, "the story of Jesus is *the* story par excellence,"[59] the primary story representing the story of the Creator.

Pastoral Care and Counseling:
Theory and Practice

Pastoral care and counseling, to maintain integrity, must be rooted in a theological anthropology that includes awareness that a person's core narratives include stories from all three dimensions of human temporality: past, present, and future. More specifically, the narrative paradigm teaches us that persons can be fully understood and effectively cared for only if the pastoral caregiver attends to their future stories. The narrative paradigm guides the minister to incorporate the future dimension of time-consciousness into pastoral care. Since the future dimension of time-consciousness provides the content and the energy for hope, a ministry that identifies the nurture of hope as a primary function must attend to the future arena of human experience.

Narrative theory informs the task of pastoral assessment by reminding us that since a person's personal identity is composed of past, present, and future stories, then cutting these future stories free does serious damage to a person's core narrative. When pastoral care specialists, following the lead of insight-oriented therapies, separate a person's past stories from present and future stories, they fail to understand the person's full narrative. Likewise, when pastoral care specialists, following the lead of therapeutic theories that emphasize present circumstances, isolate a person's present experience from past and future stories, they fail to grasp that a person's present circumstances can be effectively understood only in the context of full temporality. In either case the resulting pastoral assessment will lack the insight that can be gained from knowledge of the person's temporally complete core narrative.

Incomplete pastoral assessment, of course, means that the pastoral care and counseling strategies employed will be less effective because they will not attend to a person's future stories. In short, we can offer quality care to any individual, group, institution, or system only if we know their future stories as well as their past and present stories.

Pastoral caregivers are well trained in understanding the consequences that can result from a person's failure to appropriate the past. From clinical observation we know that a person may have ignored, forgotten, or intentionally suppressed the past for many reasons. Identity has roots in past stories that need to be recollected, organized, and connected into a coherent self-narrative. Pastoral care specialists must help persons "re-collect" and accept their past, but caregivers must also attend to the despair that comes because of a person's refusal, or inability, to confront the future and actualize the possibilities. The importance of leading people into an exploration and assessment of their future stories cannot be underestimated.

Specific cultures and cultural entities such as families and institutions, like individuals, create stories out of their experiences. When woven together, these stories, including religious stories, form core narratives that define and describe the identity of these systems. Individual stories and core narratives take shape in the context of a person's environment, the cultural nexus of family, school, church, and other such social settings. Though an individual's future stories are in their final form unique, they can be completely understood only in the cultural context.[60] Pastoral caregiving that does not consider this cultural context when assessing and intervening in future stories will not heal and nurture as effectively as counseling that understands the impact of the larger cultural narrative.

3
Future Stories and Human Brokenness

Persons in crisis were . . . caught between a hermeneutic of despair
and a hermeneutic of hope and expectation. Much of the problem
of crisis experience was . . . a loss of the sense of continuity, with
the accompanying difficulty in moving into the open-ended future
with hope and faith.
— Charles V. Gerkin, *The Living Human Document*

Narrative theory confirms that the future dimension of temporality is
structured into future stories. These future stories are integral to our
identity because they make major contributions to our core narratives.
Most important for a pastoral theology of hope, these future stories are
the stage on which we play out the dramas of hope and despair. Not
surprisingly, crises result from either real or perceived threats to the
future dimension of our core narratives. This chapter describes the connection between human brokenness and disturbances within a person's
future stories.

Brokenness and Temporality

When something "goes wrong" in life, how are we to understand
what happened? We know that to make effective interventions we need
to conceptualize the nature of the crisis. We assess the major issues and
dynamics, seeking to frame an explanation and assess the causes. The
behavioral and social sciences have developed theoretical frameworks
that offer various answers to the causation question. Every explanatory
framework includes, either explicitly or implicitly, an interpretation of
temporality. That is, any theory includes in its understanding of a crisis
assumptions about the dimension of time in which both cause and healing can be located. Psychological theories tend to focus their explanatory framework on past or present stories (see chapter 1).

Given the significance of future tense, we must realize that any problem perceived as a crisis both affects and is affected by the future stories in that person's life. No experience of suffering is completely

understandable unless we perceive how the future has been threatened, or already altered, by a past or present occurrence. As we make
pastoral assessments, awareness of breakdowns in the future dimension
of time-consciousness expands our understanding of the cause of the
suffering and offers suggestions for focusing pastoral conversation. Pastoral intervention must include attention to the lost or broken future
stories.

For the pastoral care specialist this connection of brokenness with
future tense carries additional theological consequences having to do
with hope and despair. When a future story is disturbed, then the hoping process is vulnerable to despair. Conversely, when hopelessness
overwhelms a person, then we know that something has happened to
her or his future images. A future story has been lost, stolen, abused, or
distorted by a developmental snag, a traumatic event, or any combina-
tion of life forces. Here we will examine the place of future dimensions
of time-consciousness and hope in critical life experiences.

Crisis and Future Tense

Pastoral care and counseling often occur in the context of human
dilemmas in which some external event or internal chaos unexpectedly
threatens physical, social, psychological, and spiritual stability. Definitions of crisis abound, but they all refer to a disruption in human existence that creates a higher level of anxiety than normally experienced
and throws us into a state of disequilibrium.[1] In the context of social
constructivist theory, a crisis is an event that threatens a person's existing frame of reference or worldview. Some object, person, or relationship that contributes significantly to a person's constructed reality is
lost, changed, or threatened.

Think about the following crises presented by student pastors in a
small clinical case group: a husband suddenly announces he wants a
divorce, a twenty-three-year-old son tells his family he has AIDS, a forty-
one-year-old divorcée with three young adult children discovers she is
pregnant, and a couple's fourteen-month-old daughter is diagnosed
with multiple disabilities. Obviously the major threat in these crises
comes because of the perceived changes in the future stories of these
persons.

Regardless of which dimension of time seems to provide the most
obvious explanation, any human crisis is affected by all three time
frames of human temporality. The present circumstances, of course,
provide the here and now event, the context of these crises. Certainly
past experiences provide the knowledge and experience that allow
these individuals to recognize life is going to change in negative direc-

tions. Awareness of potential future suffering, however, is the ingredient that transformed the situations into crises. At the heart of these crises is the fear and anxiety related to projected alterations of the future story. An event will not be experienced as a crisis unless some aspect of the event affects one's vision of the future in negative ways.

Narrative theory adds another metaphor for understanding the nature of crises. From the narrative perspective a crisis can be defined as a disruption in the flow of a person's core narrative, particularly the future story component. From a pastoral theological perspective, threats to one's future story make one vulnerable to despair. Past events and present circumstances certainly create the environment that makes us vulnerable and the historical context in which events and relationships threaten us. But to understand fully a human crisis, the future-tense dimensions of that situation must be explored. We must ask, How has a future story been affected? How has the not-yet been disturbed or shut down? What dark cloud has drifted over a person's horizons and made it difficult to imagine positive possibilities? Opening up positive possibilities in the future dimension of time-consciousness is necessary for the resolution of a crisis.

Case Story: Jean's "I Must Give Birth" Narrative

Let me describe a thirty-something couple—Jean is a teacher and Frank is a pastor. Their main concern has been their difficulty both in getting pregnant and in carrying a pregnancy to term. Jean's pastor referred her after a second miscarriage to explore the intense level of anxiety and depression that accompanied her grief. She and I discovered that her grief was complicated by guilt and a dismal self-concept. She worked toward understanding and redeeming the guilt and anger associated with her family of origin and an emotionally abusive first marriage. She made peace with these past stories and concentrated on establishing a new self-concept that called for differentiation from her family, a more realistic body-image, and acceptance of her skills and accomplishments as a teacher.

During our process, Jean and Frank continued working with a fertility specialist as they tried to get pregnant again. During the course of therapy, however, she intentionally dodged the issue of future stories about pregnancy and motherhood. I asked questions such as, "When will we talk about the possibility that you can't have a child of your own?" She always responded with something like, "I know we need to talk about that, but let's don't talk about it yet." Like many people, for reasons I will discuss in a later chapter, Jean was more comfortable talking about past and present stories than future stories. Summer came and we decided to bring our process to a close. Near the end of our last session we had this exchange.

> PASTORAL COUNSELOR: We never did get to the question about how you see yourself in the future if you are not able to have a child.
> JEAN: I've done a good job of ducking that question! And I appreciate your not pressing the issue.
> P.C.: Can you at least tell me why you had to duck it?
> JEAN: Simple, I can't even imagine what it would be like to not have a child. It makes me so anxious to even hear you ask that I know I must be scared to think about it. Down deep I'm afraid that if I don't have my own child, I will be a nobody.

When Jean finally did address the issue, though only in the brief interchange described above, she was clear that her hoping process was attached to motherhood. Jean's core narrative, the central drama of her personal identity, included the specific future story of having her own biological child. Younger women often have visions of motherhood as a major ingredient in their projections of future identity, of course, but difficulties in getting pregnant, two miscarriages, her age (39), and ambivalent messages from the physician had not altered Jean's core narrative. For her to have any sense of self, her future stories had to include a child. She did not think she could accept herself as a complete and competent woman without motherhood. Her self-esteem was riding on it. Because Jean was so enmeshed with the image of having her own child, she could not project a conscious future story that did not picture "mother with child." As we will see, however, several of her unconscious future stories were shaped around the fear that she would not bear a child. These stories explain some of the extra anxiety associated with her grief.

The next year Jean got pregnant for the third time but again miscarried. This time she and Frank, with whom I had done some individual counseling in the meantime, came to see me together. They shared their grief, devastation, and despair—their fear that they would never be able to complete a pregnancy. We processed the grief, which was particularly intense for Jean, and then moved into conversation about the decision concerning whether to try to get pregnant again. The physician expressed concern about their moving forward with another attempt at creating a pregnancy because they were becoming physically and psychologically exhausted.

We discussed at length two other possibilities: pursuing adoption and deciding not to have children. Frank seemed open to either option out of concern for Jean's health. Though Jean agreed rationally that either option made sense, she became increasingly anxious at any thought of halting the process of trying to get pregnant. What was the source of this anxiety? We reviewed her past and present stories to see if we could pinpoint the cause. We agreed that there were some contributions from her history, but nothing seemed to account for the extent of her anxiety. Then we began to consider her future stories.

PASTORAL COUNSELOR: Well, Jean, it looks as if we are going to have to return to the future story issue where we ended last May.

JEAN: But I don't feel that way anymore. I would feel I was O.K. even if I didn't have a baby.

P.C.: Perhaps, but let's explore the bigger question. How would having a baby change your future?

JEAN: I don't know.

P.C.: You mentioned last week that you will be making a trip to [hometown] in several weeks for Thanksgiving. Let's have a "what if" conversation about that trip, would you mind?

JEAN: All right, I'll try (*laughing*), but I know you, and you have something up your sleeve.

P.C.: Let's talk as if you were taking a newborn baby home for the first time. Picture yourself driving up to your home, and tell me what would happen.

JEAN (*she looks away and, after a pause, says*):My parents would come running out to meet us. They would be real excited and I would give over the baby to them.

P.C.: "Give over?"

JEAN: Yes, you know, like hand the baby over to them.

P.C.: It sounds like something you would do with a gift.

JEAN (*pause, a little chuckle*): Yes, like I would have had the baby for them. (*pause*) It feels like it was theirs instead of mine! (*some tears*) I guess maybe my parents would accept my child even if they don't accept me. I always thought that someday I would present them with my very own child and they would finally accept me as an adequate woman, which I never felt from them when I was growing up.

Jean went on to describe how she had fantasized that her parents would love, affirm, and bless her as a mother in a way that she had never felt loved, affirmed, and blessed as herself. Though this was a painful conversation for Jean, placing this future story on the table of consciousness was important to the healing process. This narrative was a future story by which she imagined filling a gap in her identity, gaining a blessing that would make her whole.

I suggested that Jean and Frank continue to consider what other future stories would be changed or threatened if they were unable to have their own child. At our next session Frank described how Jean had become aware of another future story. During the coming visit to their hometown, they would be spending one weekend at the church where he grew up and was ordained. They became aware, with reference to the future story question, that they would enjoy showing a new baby to the people at that church.

> JEAN: I realized when we were talking about visiting the church how happy Frank would be if he could show off his own child. I wanted Frank to be fulfilled in his desire to father a child. And then I suddenly cried and had this scary feeling that I haven't told either of you—about Frank leaving me if we couldn't have a child.
>
> P.C.: You mean divorce?
>
> JEAN: Yes, I have always thought that I better have a baby or he would find a woman that could.

Here was a second future story creating some of Jean's anxiety in the face of a decision to stop trying to get pregnant. Her perception was that for Frank to be fulfilled in the marriage he had to father a child. If she could not bear a child, she feared he would leave her for "some woman who could carry one the whole nine months." She thought she could prevent Frank's leaving by having children and feared the marriage would end if she couldn't carry a pregnancy to term. She was overwhelmed by anticipatory grief.

Further conversation about these future stories and their impact on her feelings made it clear why she could not think about adoption. Because the main reason, at unconscious levels, for having a child was to receive a blessing from her parents and keep her husband happy, the child had to be her own biological progeny. Her parents had to know that "she did it," and Frank had to know it was "his" child. In a later chapter this type of future story will be described as dysfunctional because it contributes to despair rather than hope. Becoming a birth mother is an appropriate core narrative, but when it traps a person in the present and closes down the future then it becomes an idol.

The experience of Jean and Frank helps us to understand how future stories can be at the root of personal anxiety, anticipatory grief, and interpersonal stress. Certainly Jean's future projections contained material that was rooted in her personal history and contributed to the shape of these future stories. This personal history needed to be uncovered, examined, and resolved. Future stories, however, take on a life of their own and must be confronted on their own terms. Exploration of future stories provides insight about a person's situation that is not available from simply uncovering personal history. Life-changing insight can be gained not only from stories past but also from stories future.

To comprehend holistically the hopelessness that was invading Jean's life, we had to explore both her memory and her anticipation. Effective caregiving had to include intervention in both past and future dimensions of her sense of self. The renewal of hope depended on identifying the dysfunction in her future stories and then working to reframe or reconstruct more hopeful stories. Later we will return to their situation to discuss pastoral interventions in destructive future stories.

Grief and Future Tense

The experience of grief is a common crisis confronted by pastors and chaplains. Pastoral counselors work frequently with people who have not effectively resolved a bereavement crisis. We can categorize much of what happens in bereavement as "future stories lost." This phrase describes a whole constellation of problems with future tense that pastoral care specialists must consider when making assessments and interventions in grief situations. Let's begin with a brief case study.

Case Story: Lana's Unresolved Grief

Lana is a middle-aged widow whose husband died unexpectedly several years ago. She came to the pastoral counseling center at the request of her two adult children because, as Lana says, "I haven't been the same since he died." In response to questions about her present situation, she said she "didn't care about much anymore," found herself to be "nervous a lot," would "cry a lot for no reason," and even though people asked, "she didn't want to go anywhere." She had tried hard to get over her husband's death because she knew "that God wants us all to be happy and enjoy life." Like many people (if we listen carefully), Lana introduced the hope issue by saying that God was upset with her because she was "feeling so hopeless and I know God expects Christians to be filled with hope."

Lana gave her own interpretation of why she had not recovered in this revealing statement, "I know that somewhere in my past something happened that would explain all of this if I could just find out what it was." Though not highly educated, she was familiar with the idea that any present situation can be explained definitively by childhood events. The pastoral counselor confirmed this mind-set by taking more of her history.

The pastoral counselor brought Lana's story to a case conference at which the following issues were considered. What had changed for Lana by her husband's death? What dimension of her time-consciousness had been affected by this loss? Her past stories had not changed with the death of her husband, though she had some regrets about the past to which the counselor had to be attuned. Certainly she had been enmeshed in the marital relationship and failed to develop her own sense of self. Her present story had been rudely interrupted, of course, but the time dimension that had been most disturbed was the future. Most of Lana's future stories, some of her deepest core narratives, had included traveling and grandparenting with her husband. His death had effectively destroyed these future stories. Her core narrative about marriage and family unity had come to an abrupt end—no more story. Lana's future was empty.

A pastoral assessment could describe Lana as having an unresolved grief, but describing her suffering as the loss of future story would also be accurate. After her husband's death she was unable to construct future stories that were hopeful. In theological terms, she had lost hope and fallen into despair. Her finite stories were separate from the sacred story, and she was not able to tap the hopeful resources of the Christian tradition. Effective pastoral counseling had to confront her inability or unwillingness to create hopeful future stories. In Kierkegaard's terms, she was not using her freedom to balance necessity (her husband's death and the emotional pain of this loss) with possibility (the potential for making a future without him).

The literature on loss and separation focuses more attention on what has been lost out of the past and taken from the present than on what has been lost from the future. Books on pastoral care in grief situations refer to helping the bereaved by resolving the anger and guilt that surface, repairing the wounded ego, undergirding the loss of self-esteem, and facing the fears rooted in separation anxiety developed in childhood. Clinical observation, however, clearly reveals that the most profound feelings, the most intense pain of the bereaved, lies in the loss of future stories.

Facilitating her grief work must, of course, include allowing her to tell meaningful stories about their life together (past stories). As with most people, this type of remembering is an important part of the grieving process. Most important, however, is to invite the grieving person to describe the future stories that have been lost. Separation means losing future stories, a loss that is a major aspect of bereavement. Lana, like most people, shed the most tears and expressed the heaviest sadness, when she described the future stories in which she had placed her hope, stories that had now been lost.

What do these observations contribute to the function of pastoral care in grief situations? First, early in the process when the parishioner is expressing deep grief over a loss, a pastor can provide opportunities for the bereaved to describe not only the history of the relationship but also the future stories that have been lost. I have found people quick to identify those destroyed future plans, dreams, goals, and hopes. Discovering and mourning the lost future stories is as important as remembering and rehearsing the past stories that were meaningful. Second, moving through the grief process means confronting any dysfunctional future stories that spring up in the aftermath of the loss. Third, healing involves reconstruction of future stories. Confronting dysfunctional future stories and reconstructing hopeful future stories will be described in later chapters.

Anticipatory Grief

The grief we experience prior to a specific loss, as distinguished from bereavement grief that occurs after a loss, is called *anticipatory grief*. This grief occurs when we begin to recognize and accept that we could lose, or will lose, some person, relationship, place, or object dear to us. In temporal terms, anticipatory grief obviously refers to future-tense concerns. Anticipatory grief work, then, is the process by which we prepare ourselves for a traumatic event that is rushing toward us from the future. In narrative terms, we are preparing for the loss or potential loss of a future story. In fact, anticipatory grief by definition means recognition that some important aspect of one's perceived reality, a core narrative as projected into the future, will not continue to be part of one's future story.

Caregiving during anticipatory grief, as in bereavement grief, is most effective when the person is invited to conceptualize how life will be different in the future if or when the loss occurs. Then the caregiver must enable the grieving person to slowly reframe a future story in which the lost person or object is eased out of the picture. Recovery includes constructing a revised future story that does not include that which is being lost.

Anxiety and Future Tense

The primacy of future tense in human experience of crisis can be further illustrated by taking a close look at the dynamics of anxiety. Anxiety in this section will be defined as the apprehension triggered by a perceived threat to one's self.[2] The *Diagnostic and Statistical Manual of Mental Disorders* of the American Psychiatric Association defines anxiety as the "apprehensive anticipation of future danger or misfortune [which] may be internal or external," and describes manifestations that include "apprehensive expectation, and vigilance and scanning."[3] Notice the emphasis on what *could* happen rather than what has already occurred or is taking place at the moment. Why do we experience these surges of anxiety? Anxiety can only be comprehended holistically in the context of temporality, with the emphasis on future tense.

Acute anxiety is that immediate rush of physical, cognitive, and emotional mobilization experienced in the face of a circumstance we perceive as threatening. Imagine these two common anxiety-producing situations: finding a lump in your breast or awakening at 2 A.M. to find that your fifteen-year-old is not home. An adequate explanation of the anxiety generated by these events must include all three dimensions of time.

The *present tense* would provide the immediate stimulus: feeling the lump or discovering she is not home. *Past tense*, our experience with life's realities (Kierkegaard's "actualities" and Augustine's "memories"), would provide the data and the context from which we would form our interpretations of the stimulus and immediately infuse it with meaning. We would instantaneously construct general interpretations and assign meanings typical of persons in our culture (this lump could be malignant; she could be hurt), but we also assign specific interpretations and meanings unique to our experience (my mother died of breast cancer; her date is not trustworthy).

For my purposes, of course, I must pay attention to the primacy of *future tense* in understanding the anxiety that these situations would generate. The definition of anxiety given above uses the phrases "anticipation of danger," "apprehensive expectation," and "vigilance," all of which refer to what could be coming, not to what has already occurred. The degree of anxiety would be determined by our split-second interpretation of how negatively the situation could affect our future. We perceive immediately that cancer or harm to our child could significantly alter our future stories. No anxiety would occur without this capacity to project ourselves into future suffering. Anxiety is produced by the capacity of our mind and heart immediately to imagine a future story marked by negative consequences.

Panic Attacks

Panic attacks are a type of anxiety that illustrates the role future tense plays in the human condition. Panic disorders certainly have roots in a person's past, but since they are characterized by "intense apprehension, fearfulness, or terror . . . with feelings of impending doom,"[4] we must recognize the future-tense component of this disorder.

Case Story: Leonard's Fear of Exposure

Leonard, a former student who is now a pastor, called to say he was registering for a week-long continuing education event on our campus, but his main reason for attending was to pursue counseling. We set up three appointments. At the first session he described panic attacks that occurred when he would go into the county seat town, twenty miles from his new pastorate, where his family needed to do most of their shopping. He would have unnerving symptoms when he went into the mall and certain other stores: labored breathing, suddenly "needing air," sweaty palms, and "feeling flushed and hot." Above all, he experienced a "panicky feeling that something bad was going to happen." Leonard had quit going into town except when absolutely necessary, such as to visit parishioners in the hospital. Now he was beginning to experience symptoms even when driving to the hospital. The panic attacks were leading toward a phobia.

In response to my reconnaissance questions Leonard gave me an overview of his history and his present situation. He had no history of panic attacks or other psychiatric disorders. He had been pastor in his present location for five months, was happily married with one young child, and could not identify any unusual stress. When I asked about future stories, he described some of his dreams and expectations, but nothing significant came forth. I suggested that we assume until our appointment the next day that hidden in his mind was a future story with frightening content. I asked him to do some searching for this concealed story.

The next day he returned with the story uncovered and an assessment in hand. The county seat town is the home of the junior college he had attended. For several months at the beginning of his sophomore year he had participated in homosexual behavior with four other persons who lived in his dormitory. He explained, "I wondered about my masculinity and thought this experiment would be a way to find out whether I was gay." After several months he sought help from a well-trained campus minister. After exploring his sexuality in depth he decided that his main orientation, though undeveloped, was heterosexual, and he withdrew from the sexual interactions. He remained friends with two of the group, but experienced overt suspicion and hostility from the other two, who blamed him for community awareness of their activity and the resulting alienation and conflict in the dorm. Those two had threatened to "pay him back" in the future.

When considering a move to this local church, Leonard had recalled this period in his life but had no idea it would be a problem. After arriving in town, however, he began to fantasize encountering one of those two hostile young men. Leonard imagined they would discover he was now married and a pastor. In his fantasy, their unresolved anger would be expressed by exposing his behavior to his wife and congregation. He imagined being divorced by his wife, fired by his church, and rejected by his parents, who would also find out. He had worked hard to suppress these fantasies "because they were illogical."

Leonard's future stories were a central ingredient in the anxiety attacks. Though this past story had been in his mental warehouse since college, Leonard had never experienced panic attacks until a change in present circumstances triggered the construction of a threatening future story. Effective assessment of Leonard's panic attacks involved tracking down the future story that was creating the anxiety. Likewise, pastoral intervention involved not only gaining insight into previous circumstances but helping Leonard deconstruct the dysfunctional future story and replace it with a hopeful one. I will return in later chapters to these processes.

Existential Anxiety

Psychoanalytic theory suggests that basic anxiety is rooted in and grows out of personal history, the past dimension of our lives. Such a theoretical concept certainly makes sense on the basis of clinical experience. Pastoral counselors are constantly caring for people whose present emotional struggle is related to experiences during childhood.

Existentialist psychology expands our understanding of basic anxiety by demonstrating its connection to ontological anxiety. Ontological anxiety, explains Irvin Yalom in *Existential Psychotherapy,* is rooted not in conflicts resulting from our earliest experiences but

> in conflict that flows from the individual's confrontation with the givens
> of existence . . . ultimate concerns, certain intrinsic properties that are a
> part, and inescapable part, of the human being's existence in the world.[5]

Yalom discusses anxiety related to four existential concerns: the fear of death, the search for meaning, the necessity of taking responsibility for our existence, and the dread of isolation. The uniqueness of past and present experience with both smaller systems (such as families and faith communities) and within the larger cultural context certainly influences how an individual frames these ontological issues. Furthermore, this anxiety must be confronted in the here-and-now context of our existence. However, ontological anxiety is primarily rooted in our awareness of future dimensions of temporality. Existential issues would not create anxiety if they did not reflect our awareness of future time and our capacity to project content into this future.

The deepest and most pervasive of these ultimate concerns, the grandparent of existential awareness, is finitude—the fact that we are the creatures who know at some level of consciousness that our finitude comes to an end. We will die. Anxiety about dying, obviously, does not focus on the past. This anxiety occurs in the present as we anticipate the not-yet. Death is always coming toward us from the future. Though we are accomplished at denying this reality, at existential levels this awareness is significantly affecting our future stories.

Case Story: Jason Assumes a Premature End

Jason was referred by his physician because of heart symptoms with no discernible physiological basis. He agreed to come because of his awareness that he had been fighting with depression for several months. Jason readily identified another symptom, intermittent periods of anxiety marked by sudden onset of heavy sweating, muscle tension, breathing difficulties, and "the need to escape." We examined his past and present stories and found little that was remarkable and few immediate clues about either the depression or the anxiety. As I moved to ask about future stories in the last ten minutes of this initial interview, the following conversation occurred.

> PASTORAL COUNSELOR: Jason, you have introduced me to your history and to your present circumstances, but nothing you describe immediately suggests an explanation for the depression and anxiety you have been experiencing. Tell me some stories about your future.
>
> JASON: What?
>
> P.C.: Where are you heading? What does life look like out in front of you? What stories have you created about the tomorrows?
>
> JASON (a long pause and then an ironic little laugh followed softly by this): There won't be many tomorrows. (another pause) Oh well . . .
>
> P.C.: Elaborate.
>
> JASON: It's nothing.
>
> P.C.: Could you tell me the story of this "nothing"?
>
> JASON (reluctantly): There isn't much of a story, I don't have many tomorrows, as you say, to look forward to. (pause)
>
> P.C.: Help me understand.

JASON: Well, my grandfather died of a massive stroke when he was forty-two years old. My father had a heart attack when he was forty-one and died nine months later. (*pause, and then with intensity*) Do you want to check the form I filled out? I turned forty in February [four months earlier].

P.C.: I see. So, may I ask the specifics of how this gives shape to your future story?

JASON (*with a resigned yet angry tone*): I have known all along that my heart would get me just like it got them.

P.C.: And then?

JASON (*with a trembling voice*): I'll be dead (*pause, and then in a whisper*), and I won't see my kids anymore.

P.C.: Do you have a time frame?

JASON (*with sadness and a sigh*): Early forties.

An accurate and complete assessment of Jason's situation must include the despair that permeated his existence. He was overcome with hopelessness because he perceived that a significant future story (having a long relationship with his children) was coming to an end.

The material Jason wanted to suppress was not the stories of his past and present but stories of the future. He wanted to deny that a future story of his imminent death existed, yet this story was the basic causal factor in his anxiety, including his physical symptoms. As I will demonstrate in chapter 9, changing this future story was the key to emotional, physical, and spiritual health.

Toward a Pastoral Theology

Several anthropological building blocks for a pastoral theology of hope have already been identified: (1) time-consciousness must be recognized as a basic component of the existential context of human existence; (2) future tense is a primary dimension of this temporality; (3) humans are storied creatures who, through narrative principles, develop core narratives that structure their sense of self-in-the-world; and (4) future stories are basic elements in these core narratives.

Now add another building block to a pastoral theology of hope: (5) all human brokenness is inescapably connected to disturbances in future dimensions of temporality. Though our past experience shapes our response to crisis, grief, and anxiety, the self-conscious awareness that the not-yet is either under significant threat or has been changed already creates the actual pain and suffering.

This chapter demonstrates that human brokenness is linked inseparably to problems with our future projections. Human brokenness is more completely understandable when we grasp that a major aspect of that brokenness has to do with the disruption, or the loss, or the failure of future stories. Most important for a pastoral theology of hope, this future dimension of our time-consciousness is the staging area for hope and despair. Human beings experience worry, fear, anxiety, and dread in this realm of anticipatory consciousness. The future direction of our narrative is the arena for possibility—the space in which we can plan action, solve problems, change directions, and mature.

Pastoral Care and Counseling: Theory and Practice

Ministry in crisis situations has a long history in the Christian church (as in all religions). When religious people are in crisis, they frequently seek out the pastor/priest because the suffering that attends crises raises spiritual and theological questions. Many authors have examined the existential crisis that results from the loss of the sense of the presence and providence of God. Charles Gerkin summarizes the consequences for future stories:

> Persons in crisis were caught between a hermeneutic of despair and a hermeneutic of hope and expectation. Much of the problem of crisis experience was a loss of the sense of continuity, with the accompanying *difficulty in moving into the open-ended future with hope* and faith.[6]

For this reason, Gerkin argues, a model for crisis intervention that focuses only on reestablishing stability or on solving the problem is not adequate for pastoral care and counseling.[7] He is not against stabilization and problem solving, of course, but argues that the theological issues call for pastoral care and counseling "to move beneath and beyond" these practical concerns because, as he says,

> Crisis events ... contain implications concerning the most profound questions of meaning and religious faith. ... Ultimate questions become immediate and existential in times of such crises ... questions concerning the presence or absence of God ... questions concerning the meaning of suffering, the ultimate grounding for human hope even in apparently hopeless situations.[8]

Broken future stories mean that the hoping process is threatened.

From a narrative perspective this means that a person's core narrative, the central story of her or his life, must in some manner confront existential anxiety. We have explored the inherent connection between existential anxiety and the human capacity for projecting into the future tense. In fact, if a person's core narrative is not enabling her or him

to respond to these basic anxieties, then questions must be raised about
the adequacy, indeed the basic trustworthiness, of that core narrative.

Stanley Hauerwas identifies the truthful narrative as the one that
possesses the capacity to confront existential anxiety. True narratives
"provide us with the skills to handle the basic ontological invariables
of our lives—e.g., fate, anxiety, tragedy, hope, and so on." [9] Responses
to these issues, of course, must come from the fabric of one's narrative,
which relates to the future tense. It is obvious that the pastoral care
specialist cannot adequately deal with these existential issues without
being willing to encounter future dimensions of a person's time-
consciousness, the stage on which a person's narrative plays out the
drama of hope or despair. "It is when the way ahead is cloudy," Gerkin
says, "that the hermeneutical question needs to be asked." [10] Or in my
language, when crises arise, that is definitely the time to assess future
stories. When a person is broken or wounded, we can assume that their
perceptions of the future have been invaded, altered, or threatened.
Healing can occur only if a person comes to grips with these personal
threats to her or his future stories. I will illustrate in chapter 10 how
this concern makes a difference between intervention conducted by a
pastoral counselor and a solution-oriented therapist.

Given the inherent spiritual and theological content of existential
anxiety issues, we are unfaithful to our calling and to the conscious or
unconscious needs and expectations of many parishioners/clients/pa-
tients if pastoral care does not address these frightening spiritual concerns. Pastors must remember that in any crisis intervention, a future
story needs attention. The helping process must include enabling
people consciously to face the projected future stories where brokenness has occurred. To view a crisis or a problem holistically, and to
offer the most effective interventions, pastoral caregivers must consider
the contributions of all three dimensions of time, particularly the future tense.

4
Future Stories and Hope

As plants arch their stems toward the sun, so human beings twist
from ankle to chin toward the future: not just toward a tomorrow
like today and yesterday, but toward the future that never becomes past.

—Stephen Crites, "Storytime"

Hope is for the soul what breathing is for the living organism.
Where hope is lacking, the soul dries up and withers.

—Gabriel Marcel, *Homo Viator*

Given the foundational role of future in human consciousness, how
does a person address this future dimension of temporality? Human
beings and their cultures cannot ignore the passing of time; individuals
and communities must respond in some way to the fact that the future
is coming toward them.

How a person thinks about and feels toward the not-yet is crucial to
physical, emotional, and spiritual health. The attitude one takes toward
the future can be placed on a continuum between hope and despair.
We will focus in this chapter on the connection between anticipatory
consciousness and the dynamic of hope.

Future and Hope

When constructing components of a pastoral theology of hope (chapter 1), I claimed that future consciousness was the primary tense for
hope and its opposite, despair. Yet hope should not be separated from
any dimension of temporality, because like all human experience hope
is embedded in time. However, though it has roots in the past and is
acted out in the present, hope is primarily identified with and shaped
by the future dimension of human temporality. In fact, this dimension
of our temporality which anticipates what is to come is often called our
capacity to hope. The answer to the question, What does it mean to be
human? must include our ability to hope. This ability to anticipate the
future is an ontological given, perhaps the most authentic and distinc-
tive characteristic of humanity.

Psychologist Erik Erikson understood the future dimension and its relationship to hope. True to his psychoanalytic heritage, he knew that at any given moment our personal history (past tense) plays a major role in shaping who we are. As a developmentalist, however, Erikson was always conscious that life is going somewhere, selfhood is in process toward something. He paid attention to the future schemas that influence the unfolding of human personality and identified the positive, expectant approach to these future images as hope. Erikson claimed hope as the first prerequisite for healthy development, placing it as the necessary foundation for all other human virtues: "Hope is both the earliest and the most indispensable virtue inherent in the state of being alive . . . [and] if life is to be sustained hope must remain." [1]

We referred earlier to Ernst Bloch's understanding that anticipatory consciousness was the central defining capacity of human beings. He identified this psychological process with the philosophical concept of hope and believed that hope was the central ingredient of human life. Hope in Bloch's philosophy is not only a psychological and sociological reality but a metaphysical reality, part of the structure of existence. Bloch effectively merged his ideas about the structure of reality and the nature of human existence so that he did not speak of hope only as a subjective psychological condition but as a basic ingredient of both the internal and external human condition. He understood hope not only as subjective or psychological but also as an objective ontological possibility. As a process-oriented philosopher, Bloch believed in an open future that can be shaped by human hope. Ontological structures are open to an undetermined and as yet unimaginable future that will unfold as it moves toward us.

Bloch influenced Jürgen Moltmann and the other eschatological theologians who developed the "theology of hope" in the 1960s. Though a self-professed Marxist, Bloch was interested in the theme of hope that underlies the Judeo-Christian tradition and thought that the biblical tradition supported his thesis about the future orientation of humankind. [2] Moltmann claimed that Bloch's philosophy of hope was more helpful than any other philosophical system for conceptualizing the Christian doctrine of hope.

The most noted person in psychoanalytic circles to take the future orientation of human beings seriously was Viktor Frankl. He learned about the importance of a person's attitude toward the future from his experience in a concentration camp. He discovered that hope was the primary emotional ingredient in the survival of his fellow prisoners. Frankl's description of his hope of publishing his theories on psychoanalysis, and the role this hope played in his survival, has been widely read. [3]

Frankl disagreed with those who claimed that human beings are determined primarily by drives and instincts. He developed concepts such as the "will to meaning" that describe human beings as reaching toward the future for meaning and fulfillment. He refers to this "will to meaning" as the "basic striving" of human beings.[4] Irvin Yalom provides a concise summary of Frankl's perspective:

> Frankl is careful to distinguish between drives . . . that push a person from within . . . and meaning . . . that pulls a person from without. . . . The difference is between drive and strive. In our most essential being, in those characteristics that make us most human rather than animal, we are not driven but instead actively strive for some goal. "Striving" conveys a future orientation: we are pulled by what is to be, rather than pushed by relentless forces of past and present.[5]

Gabriel Marcel, a French philosopher who also was fascinated by the significance of hope to human beings, believed hope was the driving force that enabled humans to move into the future dimension of time-consciousness. Marcel's ideas about this process of existence were expressed through the metaphor of journey. He believed humans are travelers on a pilgrimage, that "we can say with supreme truth that 'being' necessarily means 'being on the way' (en route)."[6] His journey metaphors include our consciousness of future time, and Marcel anticipates narrative theory in these words: "All human life develops in the manner of a drama."[7] Journey implies being in motion toward a destination, having a starting point, and projecting a finishing point. If you are on a journey, particularly if you consider it a pilgrimage, then "where you are now" is not "where you are going." The destination must be imaged in the future story.

What is the engine that provides the energy for this journey? For Marcel, hope is the driving force, the underlying dynamic that pulls humans into the future. The essence of this journey is the process of moving toward a more authentic expression of human existence, which from Marcel's perspective involves progression toward transcendence. Marcel, as a theist, believed that the final destiny of the human journey is participation in the transcendent being of God.

Marcel came to these conclusions about hope from phenomenological observations about the nature of human existence. He saw that hope—both mundane hopes of everyday existence and metaphysical hopes—is present in almost every action initiated by people. He believed, like Bloch, that the capacity for these small acts of hoping implies a more profound ground of hope that lies beyond the human condition.

What Is Hope?

Developing an inclusive and adequate definition of hope is difficult. John Macquarrie says that hope "is a diffuse, inclusive concept, denoting a mood or an attitude in which beliefs, emotions, imagination and purpose are all combined . . . characterized by a measure of confidence and affirmative expectation about the future."[8] Words found in a dictionary or a thesaurus to describe hope include trust, expectation, desire, promise, confidence, assurance, anticipation, and conviction. Theologian David Woodyard describes the attitude and potential of hope:

> What is most authentic about [humans beings] is the disposition to hope, to live from the future rather than in terms of the past and present. In hoping, [humanity] reaches beyond every apparent limit with anticipation, inquiry, and vision. . . . Hope is not the calculation of a new future based on extrapolations from present data; it is a confidence that the unpredictable will happen. The most fundamental consciousness . . . is a passionate longing for what is "not yet." When [humans beings are] truly in possession of [their] existence, [they] experience the process of hoping as a militant aspiration for something new in the future.[9]

When speaking of hope, I am addressing the configuration of cognitive and affective responses to life that believes the future is filled with possibilities and offers a blessing. Used theologically, the word *hope* describes a person's trusting anticipation of the future based on an understanding of a God who is trustworthy and who calls us into an openended future. This God keeps promises of deliverance, liberation, and salvation.

How is hope related to our experience of the future? In each present moment hope is anticipating the next moment, the next step—responding to the thought of tomorrow with expectation, even excitement! Theologian William Lynch describes hope as

> the fundamental knowledge and feeling that there is a way out of difficulty, that things can work out, that we as human persons can somehow handle and manage internal and external reality, that there are 'solutions' in the most ordinary biological and physiological sense of that word, that above all, there are ways out.[10]

Hope is committed to the future. People who hope perceive themselves to be on a pilgrimage, on a journey into tomorrow. As Karl Menninger says, "[hope] implies a process . . . a going forward, a confident search."[11] Hopers are always leaving one level of experience, awareness, knowledge, insight, and/or wisdom and moving to another level, another stage. Hope remembers that the present moment is coming at us from a future filled with possibilities. As expressed by Stephen Crites, "the future is the universal fluidity from which everything new is born. . . . [A]ll new things come into existence out of the future." [12]

The Hoping Process

How does this capacity for hope develop? How do human beings shape the ontological reality of anticipatory consciousness into the gift of hope? Projecting ourselves into the future dimension by developing future stories is a natural process, but what gives hopeful content and tone to these stories?

Narrative Perspectives

Development of anticipatory awareness comes early in life (see chapter 2). We are very young when we begin looking into the not-yet through our anticipatory consciousness and considering possibilities. We fill this future dimension with content based on previous experience but creatively enhanced and shaped by our imagination.

I use the phrase "hoping process" to describe what happens as our capacity for envisioning the future dimension of existence attaches itself to particular content. The hoping process, of course, takes place through narrative structuring. We constantly develop future stories that express our anticipations of the future and, therefore, our hope.

A phenomenological approach to human experiences with hope makes it clear that the capacity to hope reaches into an open-ended future on the one hand and looks for specific content in concrete objects, events, and relationships on the other. I will risk oversimplification for the sake of more concrete thought and suggest that there are two categories of hope: finite hope and transfinite hope.

Finite Hope

Being finite creatures, we invest our hope in finite objects, desires, and processes. We form future stories that express our hope for a pay raise, acceptance into a certain school, a good grade, a positive word from an inquiry, winning the game, an upturn in the stock market, and other concrete, everyday content. We also hope for more important things: that the children will arrive safely, that the war will end, and that justice will prevail. In survival situations the hopeful stories might be attached to finding food, getting a job, surviving the bombs, or escaping a molesting adult.

Our language demonstrates that the hoping process focuses on objects. *Hope* is not a word we normally use without attaching it to something specific. When we use *hope* as a verb, the structure of our thought calls for some object. When we start a statement with the words "I hope that . . ." then we will finish with something specific to hope for or to hope in. "I hope that we can finish," or "We hope they can find us," or "I am hoping the pain will stop soon." Even when we use the word *hope* as a noun, we normally give it some content by connecting it to some activity, event, or object: "We have hope of making contact," or "This is our only hope!" or "Chemotherapy is our best hope."

When research psychologists speak of hope, they are referring to this finite hope. Psychologists assume that some motivation is necessary to explain human action. Ezra Stotland, a social psychologist, is willing to identify and explain this ingredient as "hopefulness" and constructs a theory of hope. Stotland summarizes different definitions of hope used by research psychologists in these words: "The essence of these meanings of hope is an expectation greater than zero of achieving a goal." In his study of hope the definitions are limited by the need to quantify, so they focus on specific "desires" and "expectations." He concludes, "*Hope* can therefore be regarded as a shorthand term for an expectation about goal attainment." [13] Stotland defends his use of a subjective term like *hope* even though researchers have difficulty developing valid measures of hopefulness. He goes on to declare that hopefulness is "a necessary condition for therapy to be effective." [14]

Transfinite Hope

I am using the word *transfinite* to describe hope that is placed in subjects and processes that go beyond physiological sensing and the material world. Along with the potential for investing our hope in everyday, finite content, we also have the potential for investing in transfinite ideas and concepts. Some believe that all hope moves toward the transfinite. Marcel says, "Hope . . . tends inevitably to transcend the particular objects to which it at first seems to be attached." He goes on to describe real hope as that hope which is related not to specific objects at all, but to "ontic states" such as freedom and deliverance. [15]

Macquarrie also argues that the existence of simple hopes is a precursor of a more universal hope that expands outward from any individual to encompass loved ones, then all humans, and finally the whole world. This universal hope argues for the existence of a "transcendent reality (God) whose transcendent being is the goal that draws out our human transcendence." [16]

We need specific research on hope from the perspective of faith development, but our capacity to hope in an open-ended future must develop along with other aspects of our consciousness of future time. Early clues about how to view the future are passed on from one's family of origin and cultural context. Erikson believes that hope develops out of trusting relationships with caregivers who communicate "an all-enveloping world-image tying past, present, and future into a convincing pattern of providence." [17] Notice the emphasis on all dimensions of temporality at the heart of this statement.

Imagining an open-ended future is basic to maintaining hope. The deepest level of hope is an open-ended, trusting stance toward existence that perceives a future horizon that transcends the finite hopes expressed in our specific objectives. Transfinite hope embraces the mystery and excitement of open-ended future and the not-yet. Erikson says,

> Hope, once established as a basic quality of experience, remains independent of the verifiability of "hopes," for it is in the nature of [human] maturation that concrete hopes will . . . prove to have been quietly superseded by a more advanced set of hopes . . . [and] a greater capacity for renunciation . . . [as one] learns to dream what is imaginable and to train [one's] expectations on what promises to prove possible.[18]

When the horizons of our vision extend indefinitely, there are always possibilities and hope is more secure.

Transfinite hope is invested in sources that transcend the human condition, related to what Marcel calls "the Beyond." Philosophers and theologians alike have claimed that our capacity to hope is at the root of spiritual experience.[19] They have theorized that the future tense of human temporality is the dimension of finitude most clearly related to the development of religion.[20] Such meaningful hope must have deep roots and be communicated through sacred stories (chapter 2). Every religious tradition has sacred stories. What is the sacred story in which Christian hope is rooted? What does Christian theology bring to the future questions, What happens next? and Where is this life going?

Hope in the Judeo-Christian Tradition

Ultimately the foundation of hope in the Judeo-Christian tradition is rooted in the character of God, the Creator and Redeemer of the universe. The covenant revealed God's character to the Hebrew people and their perceptions were confirmed by God's mighty acts, such as the exodus. The followers of Jesus perceived further revelation about the nature of God. Their hope assumed certain truths about God's character because of what was revealed in the life, death, and resurrection of the carpenter from Nazareth.

What is God's character? What have our religious experiences and our understanding of the gospel taught us about God's personhood? We believe that the God who creates and sustains is primarily characterized by love, agape. The creation and the incarnation reveal the nature of this self-giving love. Macquarrie claims that "the presence and activity of God in Christ, seen as the focus and culmination of a presence and activity that extend throughout the created world, . . . is the ground of Christian hope." [21] Jesus Christ is the visible expression of God's faithfulness to our relationship and gives us reason to hope for the not-yetness of our future.

This God who loves us more than we can imagine is trustworthy and keeps promises. God is steadfast and insists on loving us despite our continued inability and/or unwillingness to respond with appropriate trust, obedience, and faithfulness. Our hope is in our relationship with this trustworthy God whose character is marked by a faithful, steadfast love for us. God is on our side! God is a loving, gracious creator and redeemer whom we can trust with the future. As the Lord told Jeremiah, "For surely I know the plans I have for you, . . . plans for your welfare and not for harm, to give you a future with hope" (Jer. 29:11).

Transfinite Hope Validates Finite Hope

Is there some connection between finite hopes and the Christian hope? I suggest that transfinite hope undergirds and informs finite hope. Hope is our creaturely response to the Creator upon whom we cannot make demands. Because this hope grows out of our experience of God's love, because it is born out of this trusting relationship, we do not need to reach for specifics and concrete certitude. Our security is in the relationship and not the particular events. Trusting in the character of God frees us from investing our deepest hope in specific objects, events, or processes.

Beyond this truth, however, we must admit with Marcel that the very nature of love is to expect something.[22] Love is characterized by expectation and anticipation of what love gives to relationships. This expectancy is based on mutual giving and receiving—quite a different dynamic than demands, or obligations, or "shoulds" and "oughts." Hope includes the excitement of imagining the potentialities in loving relationships and participating in causing these possibilities to happen!

Those of us who believe that the seeds of the realm of God are already sown among us, who believe God suffers with us, who believe the creation is groaning in travail, feel comfortable proclaiming not only liberation and freedom in the beyond but transformation within finitude, within the now. We believe that God wants abundant life, justice, and mercy to be part of life in the present. This hope is one reason that the existence of suffering is such a basic spiritual problem and why theodicy is such a thorny theological issue.

As Christians we have hope in God and the future that God is in the process of creating. In fact, this transfinite hope gives us the courage to commit ourselves to finite causes such as bringing justice into the world. We can accept that penultimate hopes, such as establishing peace, eradicating poverty, saving the environment, overcoming racism and sexism, and so forth will not be accomplished in our lifetime. Hope gives us the confidence that working toward these finite goals is meaningful because this finite hope is rooted in transfinite hope. Transfinite hope inspires and motivates because it acknowledges a future that goes beyond our finite vision. Erikson said, "All in all, then, maturing hope not only maintains itself in the face of changed facts—it proves itself able to change facts, even as faith is said to move mountains." [23]

Connecting Finite Hopes and Transfinite Hope

Ideally we keep our finite hopes in the context of our transfinite hope, our sacred story. Dietrich Ritschl wrote that our "ultimate hope" is in God's final fulfillment of promise, but this transfinite hope allows people to have "time-bound little hopes." [24] Ultimate hope allows little hopes that can be concrete. This ultimate hope can be found in finite hope because finite hope contains the signs of God. Finite hope is connected to the sacred story. When we attach our hoping process to specific content, such as vocational accomplishments, the safety of our children, or surviving a disease, we strive not to allow these goals to replace our transfinite hope in the character and activity of God. Rather we can hope in these finite goals *because* of our transfinite hope, not *instead* of our transfinite hope.

Finite hope is penultimate. We can hope securely only in the context of a transfinite hope that provides emotional and spiritual sanctuary when the goal or object of finite hope is not reached or does not materialize. When we have no horizon of open-ended future behind specific goals, we are vulnerable to despair. Christians have "hope beyond hope" and are not unduly threatened when their finite hopes do not materialize. This is one meaning of the Romans passage, "For in hope we were saved. Now hope that is seen is not hope. For who hopes for what is seen? But if we hope for what we do not see, we wait for it with patience" (Rom. 8:24–25). We do not move into despair when we lose a finite hope because we have not lost our basic, foundational, transfinite hope. We do not have to be afraid to fail, for ultimate hope is open-ended.

Roy Fairchild critiques Stotland's emphasis on attainment of goals, pointing out that finite hope invested in finite goals will be disappointed at some juncture unless backed by a transfinite hope that is not invested in objects.[25] In the words of Jesus, "Do not worry about your life, what you will eat or what you will drink, or about your body, what you will wear" (Matt. 6:25). Anxiety over the future makes it difficult to live fully in the present. Hope must be grounded in trust that the God-who-is-love will keep the promises made, rather than in expectation that God will initiate certain events or actions.

Those who anticipate deliverance and fulfillment in the future do not have to find ultimate meaning in the present. The present moment, therefore, cannot dominate the scene because hopers have a future story that communicates a future that can be different, filled with possibilities. Since hope is not ultimately placed in the present, hopers do not have to make the present ultimate.

Kurt Lewin was one of the first to demonstrate that life is contextual. Everything occurs in what he called a "field," which includes our temporality. Lewin describes our image of future time, which he calls "psychological future," as that aspect of our psychological context which has to do with hope.[26] His central purpose is to explain that our psychological future affects our perceptions of, and function in, the present. This is particularly true in the context of trouble, because hopeful anticipation about the future can alleviate suffering. "If we expect something in the future, if we have hope, we actually suffer less."[27]

In any crisis or facing any tragedy, those with hope more easily wait for the present to pass because they trust the future. They believe, This too shall pass. Tomorrow will bring surprises, things could change. In the context of bereavement, David Switzer describes hope as "the possibility and openness toward the meaningfulness of the future which keeps faith alive and active in the present."[28] Because people filled with hope have a worldview that transcends the present moment, they are expectant in the present.

The relative dominance of either hope or hopelessness sets a context for ethical behavior. John Navone, a narrative theologian, points out that a person's perception of the future, which includes her or his "vision" (what we are calling "future stories"), permeates every aspect of present existence. He says, "Our vision gives rise to our character, to our style of life, to the tone of our being in the world."[29] He uses the word "vision" in the same way I use "future story." When he claims that vision is connected to feelings, particularly compassion, and the resulting action, the same is true for future stories. Navone believes that the quality of a person's vision, or future hope, is revealed in that individual's feelings and actions in the present. To the extent that a person's future story is hopeful, then that person will feel compassion and act accordingly, and to the extent that the future story is hopeless, then compassion and the actions it prompts will be lacking. For hopers the present is pregnant with possibilities, a perception that allows them to feel purposeful.

Christian love is made possible by hope. Love is excited about the here and now, but this excitement is attached to anticipation about the tomorrows. Love is characterized by the opening up of possibility and the desire for what is potential in a loving relationship. Douglas Meeks summarized, "Hope is thus the key to the meaning of human existence and to the transformation of the present." [30] If the future seems closed, it is difficult to love in the present.

Pastoral Theological Reflection

Our culture tends to think of time only sequentially, or in linear fashion, thereby dividing the past, present, and future from each other. Biblical concepts of time, however, connect past and future to the present. Both history and eschatology are seen and experienced in the here and now. "Hope binds time and unites past and future in the present," says Robert Carrigan. God is involved in the present from both a past and future perspective. Hope "is a here and now experience that contains both a pledge of 'things to come' and 'first fruits' that can be tasted now." [31] What God has done and will do are both represented in God's presence and activity in the "eternal now." The gospel describes a God who has certainly been present and active in the past and is present with us today, but (most importantly) this God is out in front of us calling us, inviting us, into the future. God is unquestionably here with us in the present, but God reaches into the present from the future.

The Christian faith has always been teleological, believing that the creation is in process. History is going somewhere, en route to a destination, becoming something new. God is at work giving shape to the future and out in front of us calling us into this future. God "is the power of the future activating the potentialities of the present," Woodyard says. [32] This understanding of God allows believers to adopt an anticipating consciousness that is energized by hope rather than deadened by despair.

Even when events are chaotic, Christians believe that God is immanently involved in the process. The God who has a hand in the chaos is trustworthy. Humans participate in the ongoing creative process by choosing direction as individuals and communities. By interacting with our activity, God's possibilities are introduced. We do not know the final shape of things to come, nor do we know the specifics of the ending; but we can trust the One who is trustworthy, who is steadfastly engaged with this becoming.

Navone gives special attention to travel stories that express religious experience. He uses the travel stories in scripture to illustrate the narrative quality of individual religious life and to demonstrate that "the Christian community throughout the course of history, with the Risen Christ as its ultimate horizon, embraces the travel story of its Lord's self-transcendence as its own hope and promise."[33] The word "horizon" here alludes to the "out in front of us" nature of the Christian pilgrimage toward hope and promise. Hope is always moving toward what it can barely see, but yet trusts.

The Bible is filled with images of exodus, people willing to leave one place and journey over uncharted regions with the assumption that God will be their guide. Abraham is an example of the adventuresomeness of hopers, their willingness to take risks, as in Heb. 11:8: "he set out, not knowing where he was going." The concept of journey suggests intentionality about the future based on trust, even when the end is not in sight. Moltmann says that faith means

> leaving the dwelling places of reality where one has peace and security and giving oneself over to the course of history, to the way of freedom and danger, the way of disappointment and surprise, borne along and led solely by God's hope."[34]

William Lynch calls hope "an arduous search for a future good of some kind that is realistically possible but not yet visible."[35]

Christian hope expects things to be different in the future. It anticipates transformation, redemption, reconciliation, healing, salvation, deliverance. These are some of the concepts by which Christians describe their expectations of what the future holds in store, what God's promises are all about.

Pastoral Care and Counseling

One way of assessing the relative presence or absence of hope is to evaluate whether a person is on a journey in life. Does she move into new experiences, new understandings? Does he journey from one level of consciousness to another? One type of exodus is the internal, intrapsychic process of individuation and differentiation. Through these processes, an individual's sense of self emerges—a self connected to, yet distinct from, that of parents and community. The pastor, then, can be helpful in leading people on an exodus journey. To be effective, of course, the pastor must also be participating in such a journey.

Remember that if a person's travel story is aimed only at a specific, finite goal, then trouble lies ahead. Valid hope must exist in the context of a transfinite hope and focus on the open-ended horizon. Finite goals are appropriate, even necessary, for the Christian as an expression of living out one's Christian commitments in the present. Ideally, however, these hopes should not block or overshadow the transcendent horizon. If we can see and trust the open-ended, transcendent horizon in the distance, failure to reach a concrete goal will not plunge us into despair because our deeper, more pervasive hope is in what lies beyond this horizon.

Pastoral care and counseling has as one of its goals the nurture of hope, so one of its responsibilities is attending to the hoping process. Specific strategies of pastoral caregiving with people in crises must therefore focus on opening up the future. We are responsible for helping people evaluate their travel story, identify where they are going, and assess the adequacy of their horizons for supporting hope.

This whole concept of horizons, of ultimate hope, distinguishes pastoral care and pastoral counseling from methods of therapy that are only problem-oriented, or solution-oriented. (An example is given in chapter 10.) The pastoral theology of hope that undergirds and informs our task will not let us be satisfied with solving a specific problem. This pastoral theology demands that we ask questions about, and listen intently for, a person's ultimate concerns. What is the larger story, the core narrative, that provides the context in which the problem arises? What is the future story that lies beyond any given solution? What is the overarching vision in which the person is experiencing the problem? Does that vision suggest the solution? Does it provide hope of abundant life even if there is no finite solution? If not, then that vision is inadequate, and fixing the problem without attending to the need for a more functional vision of the future is "Band-Aid" care at best. Without a horizon of open-ended future, hopelessness will return.

5

Future Stories
and Despair

Despair is an ultimate or "boundary-line" situation. One cannot go
beyond it. Its nature is indicated in the etymology of the word
despair: without hope. No way out into the future appears. Nonbe-
ing is felt as absolutely victorious.

—Paul Tillich, *The Courage to Be*

Unless we can tap the sources of hope, there can be no human
future.

—Ross Fitzgerald, *The Sources of Hope*

If the capacity to hope is an ontological given, a potentiality that exists
from infancy in every human being, then the possibility of its loss or
corruption is also present from the beginning. Or, as Joan Nowotny declares, "The conditions that make it possible to hope are strictly the
same as those that make it possible to despair." [1]

Our hoping process is thus vulnerable to attack. Hopelessness is like
an infection that invades a person's being and causes a sickness of the
spirit. Despair is a serious spiritual disease with ramifications for every
aspect of our existence. I use the word *despair* to describe disturbances
of the "hoping process" in which our capacity to hope is lost, blocked,
distorted, or in some manner impaired.

Despair and Clinical Depression

The reader might well ask whether I am using the word *despair* as a
synonym for depression. Certainly depressive states and despair overlap, but I am using the terms separately in this work. When we use the
word *depression* in pastoral care and counseling, we are usually referring
to a specific psychiatric condition. Depression is identified in the current edition of the *Diagnostic and Statistical Manual of Mental Disorders*
as a disturbance of mood, which is defined as "depressed, sad, hopeless,
discouraged, or 'down in the dumps.'" [2] Clinical depression is diagnosed
when a majority of the following symptoms are present: a depressed
mood, including tearfulness, irritability, and anxiety; loss of interest in
activities that once brought pleasure; significant weight loss or gain with
decreased or increased appetite; insomnia or hypersomnia; psycho-

motor agitation or retardation; fatigue or loss of energy; feelings of worthlessness or inappropriate guilt; diminished ability to think or concentrate; thoughts of suicide or death.[3] Note that "hopelessness" is not listed as a symptom for any major depressive disorder except dysthymia.[4]

To distinguish between clinical depression and despair, I have found the following observations helpful. Despair often permeates a person's existence even when the symptoms listed above are not present. Despair can exist, even in its most desperate forms, without disturbances of eating and sleeping, without a change in energy levels or psychomotor functioning, and without any impairment in thinking processes. Sometimes symptoms can be misunderstood. A despairing person may feel helpless, for example, not because of any lack of personal power, but because he or she feels that no activity can be imbued with meaning.

The two get tangled symptomatically and are not always easy to tell apart. The symptom of hopelessness can be a major piece of the puzzle. I have found, generally speaking, that the sense of hopelessness is more specific in depression and more pervasive or universal in despair. Furthermore, clinical depression seems to be more specific in its attachment to here-and-now losses and disappointments; despair seems to be attached to a more universal loss of meaning and disillusionment with life.

From a philosophical perspective, clinical depression often occurs without changing a person's frame of reference, whereas despair seems to operate in a context in which a person's worldview has suffered a major breakdown. When this disillusionment is primarily related to the future dimension of life, despair is even more likely. Though clinically depressed persons often feel helpless about the future and may think about it negatively, despairing persons have a more philosophically nuanced ability to describe a future void of meaning.

Finally, depressed persons often experience a sense of personal worthlessness expressed through shame and guilt. Despairing persons, however, often have little negative affective responses to their own selfhood. Their cognitive perceptions are rooted in a negative assessment of the environment, as that environment projects into the future, rather than in negative self-evaluation. Clinical depression usually responds well to psychiatric and psychotherapeutic interventions, whereas despair is more resistant.

In summary, despair may include depressive moods, but despair is primarily related to a cognitive and affective response to philosophical/spiritual problems rooted in or leading to negative perceptions about the future. Despair is an internal frame of reference convinced that the future is closed down, unchangeable, or meaningless. Despair is one of the possible conclusions reached by the hoping process, a potential interpretation of the future reached by our anticipatory consciousness.

Though despair can certainly push someone into a clinical depression, and conversely, a difficult clinical depression can make one vulnerable to despair, they are not identical. Furthermore, clinical depression, even when related clearly to physiological factors, is often a symptom of despair. When pastoral caregivers treat depression as a separate entity, they may miss the main significance of the depression. The depression may mask a conscious or unconscious core narrative that cannot answer effectively an existential or spiritual question. Effectively treating the symptom is imperative, of course, but we must not assume that overcoming the depression means that the root problem has been solved. From a pastoral theological perspective, one must always pursue the possibility that the underlying issue is despair. Such sensitivity will alert us to potential future-tense concerns that could be embedded consciously or unconsciously in that person's worldview.

Pastoral theologians and pastoral care specialists have much work to do on identifying the distinctions between clinical depression and despair. My offerings above are observations gleaned from therapeutic journeys—a few suggestions for such an inquiry rather than definitive descriptions based on careful research. Now I turn to further descriptions of despair that have helped people on the therapeutic journey.

Contributors to Despair

The presence of despair prompts us to ask what goes wrong with the hoping process. Where does hopelessness come from? Why do people become hopeless? To answer these questions we will discuss eight basic contributors to despair, each with a basic reference to time-consciousness, particularly the future dimension.

Loss of Future Story

Grief has been cited (chapter 3) as an example of crises that were primarily defined by the change in a person's view of the future. Given our constant projections into the future and investment of hope in specific content, it is not surprising to learn that one cause of despair is the loss of future story. This is particularly so when the loss is sudden and traumatic, as in the unexpected death of a loved one, an announcement from out of the blue that a spouse wants a divorce, or failing to get admitted to graduate school.

A major change in circumstances significantly alters a future story.

After I preached a sermon on future stories, a couple in their fifties approached me with a brief story. They had recently learned that their twenty-seven-year-old son, an only child they adopted in their late thirties, and in whom they have made a heavy emotional and financial investment, had AIDS and was already in the latter stages of this disease. Suddenly the hopes that they had for his future were shattered, or as she described it, "Our future story has been fractured."

Despairing persons have usually lost something or someone and are suffering from prolonged, delayed, or unresolved grief—often a series of griefs. Working through grief about all one's losses and potential losses in life is certainly germane to the recovery of hope. Walter Brueggemann stresses the importance of dealing with grief and pain in order to move on with hope. He says that Jeremiah became "profoundly a prophet of hope" out of his own pain and grief.[5] Only because Jeremiah experienced his grief fully and was willing to express it to others could he become hopeful. Likewise, Jesus could weep at the tomb of Lazarus and on the hill overlooking Jerusalem, thereby grounding his communication of hope in the realities of mourning. Despairing people are often those who have been unwilling to face, express, and live through their grief and loss. The enemies of hope include silence and repression. Hope emerges among those who publicly deal with their suffering related to significant losses.

Reaching the End of a Future Story

Some people experience the beginning of despair when they reach the end of a future story in which they were extensively invested, and no other future story has been put in its place. In certain life situations a person might experience what friends and family call depression when actually the experience is a taste of despair. For example, you have finally finished a major, time- and energy-consuming project, such as graduating with an advanced degree, completing a writing project, being certified or accredited, or passing professional board exams. Then, after a celebration, you find yourself despondent. What has happened? The future story that carried you so long is now history. What is left?

Sometimes a person moves toward despair because hope was so totally invested in one particular accomplishment that other future stories were not developed. When there is no more future story, life becomes scary and one despairs. Aging persons face the constant loss of future stories as spouses, friends, and family (even adult children) die, as the ability to participate in meaningful tasks ceases, and as loss of bodily functions focuses attention on debilitation.

Another process that brings people to the end of a future story occurs when their primary future story is no longer effective, no longer provides hope. Pastoral work often begins when someone has lost faith in a future story. She or he is in the process of giving up the future story because it is producing not happiness but unhappiness, not satisfaction but dissatisfaction. In short, the future story is producing not hope but despair. Giving up a future story, no matter how dysfunctional, feels threatening because of the void left in the future tense of one's life. Living between future stories is a vulnerable time.

Pastoral care and counseling must attend to those who are running out of future story. Creative interventions focus on enabling persons to recognize the vacuum created when they accomplish or give up a future story. We represent the God who at any moment is calling us into a new future.

Not Willing to Be a Self

Kierkegaard connected the existence of a self with temporality through the concepts of "actuality" and "possibility" (chapter 1). He identified a person's actuality (or necessity) with that which already exists, the finite limitations that make up the physical, social, and psychological realities. Possibility, the potential for change and newness, is also a part of the reality inherent in each person. Possibility is the component of the self that can develop only in the future. Achievement of authentic selfhood comes from maintaining equilibrium between these two aspects of self: actuality and possibility. As Kierkegaard said, "The task of selfhood is to establish equilibrium among components of the self, or to manage time properly."[6]

The present tense provides the self with the "freedom" and responsibility to actualize the possibilities, though these can occur only within the parameters dictated by actuality. When the self does not hold these two components of self in balance, and a state of disequilibrium ensues, then that person is living an inauthentic existence and is vulnerable to despair. Kierkegaard declared, "A self which has no possibility is in despair, and so in turn is the self which has no necessity."[7]

Despair for Kierkegaard, then, is being "not willing to be one's self" and has two forms: "despair of possibility" and "despair of necessity." "Despair of possibility" results when the self is unable, or unwilling, to recognize the limitations of actuality. The self fantasizes, dreams, and wishes itself into the future in ways that are too removed from the givens of life to be realistic. "Possibility outruns necessity," Kierkegaard said, and when that happens "the self runs away from itself."[8] It seems that everything is possible; no boundaries are established.

With no realistic boundaries and faced with too much possibility, the self is unable to make decisions. The freedom to make choices and take action is lost in endless possibilities. This state of mind could be characterized as a despair of volition. One's capacity to will something is paralyzed. Since every imaginable possibility seems available, one feels helpless to choose. A person who cannot choose is unable to act.

Kierkegaard's second form of despair, the "despair of necessity," is the loss of possibility, the blindness to the open-endedness of the future.[9] This despair results when a person is buried in the givens of life, feels bound by what already exists, and has lost the willingness and freedom to imagine other alternatives. Fatalism is a common manifestation of this type of despair: whatever will be will be. In fatalism, or any type of determinism, everything coming from the future is seen as already preordained and therefore untouchable by human decision and action.

Failure to Claim Past and Future

We have established that hope is connected to all three dimensions of time-consciousness. Stephen Crites makes the point that "re-collecting" the past is foundational to self-identity and "pro-jecting" into the future is necessary for self-transcendence. Both "re-collecting" and "pro-jecting," particularly projecting positive future stories, are necessary for the self to manifest hope. One cause of despair, therefore, is a person's refusal to claim either the past or the future dimension of her or his narrative, or perhaps both. Crites argues that for persons to be happy and hopeful, that is, to have a deep sense of joy and well-being, they must have "psychic strength," which

> includes both a strong sense of self-identity, rooted in the past, and an equally strong power of self-transcendence, directed toward the future. This strength must be concentrated in the present, which is the point of tension between self-identity and self-transcendence.[10]

Obviously, as Crites says, "Despair is the refusal of either self-identity or self-transcendence."[11] The despairing person cannot or will not hold these two aspects of selfhood—past and future—in tension within the present. This type of despair Crites described as

> the failure to pro-ject myself hopefully into the future. I cannot . . . fail to have a future, but I can ignore or actively resist its claim and live from day to day without any projective scenario, or I can devote all my energy to protecting and reiterating the identity I have recollected out of the past. In either case I live without risk and without hope, doing only what is necessary to subsist more or less in the manner to which I am accustomed.[12]

For our purposes, note the despair created by the refusal, or inability, to claim the future, to actualize the possibilities in self-transcendence and hope.

Another way of conceptualizing this failure to claim the future is to describe despair as a "capitulation" to a perception of the future that is filled with negativity (a particular dysfunctional future story). Gabriel Marcel believes that the nature of the despairing act is to capitulate in the face of what appears inevitable. A person capitulates when he or she "renounces the idea of remaining my self" [13] and gives in to a loss of inner coherence and self-congruence. People who despair generalize from a particular piece of data that the future is worthless. In contrast, people who refuse to allow hope to be destroyed by the seemingly inevitable maintain the integrity of the self. As Nowotny describes Marcel's idea, "Hope, in so far as it is an active battle against despair, is a refusal of fatalism, an active non-capitulation." [14]

Being Present-Bound

Hopelessness for some people is being trapped by the present with no anticipation of tomorrow, or at least not a tomorrow that can bring relief. Being boxed in by the perception that time is going nowhere is a major characteristic of despair. In his phenomenology of hope, Marcel describes this sense that time is closed instead of open to possibilities:

> Despair seems to me above all the experience of closing or, if you like, the experience of "time plugged" up. The [one] who despairs is the one whose situation appears to be without exit . . . as if the despairer kept hitting against a wall, the wall being faceless certainly, and yet hostile, and the result of this shock or impact is that [one's] very being starts to disintegrate or, if you like, to give up. [15]

Words like "drudgery" and "boredom" describe life in the present when there is no meaningful future that promises anything new or different. People infected by hopelessness perceive the present as sterile, unable to produce or give birth to anything.

Hopelessness for many people results from their perception that the future does not hold any new thing. We can easily forget that the present moment is coming toward us from a future filled with possibilities. Individuals who experience life as a series of disappointments can fall into despair if they perceive that the future will only be a repetition of the same negative events. When these negative experiences are projected into the future, they become the basis for dysfunctional future stories. Lynch calls this the feeling of "endlessness," the sense that nothing can change. Such a picture of endless repetition within a person's future stories is a major cause of hopelessness.

Anticipatory consciousness, then, sees the future only as a mirror of what has already happened. Nowotny says, "The despairing [person] anticipates nothing but the eternalization of [her or his] present situation. . . . The future appears as a negation, an anticipation of future failure, and thus appears to be . . . an 'absence of exit.'"[16] Crites says, "Hell is the ceaseless reiteration of the past: abandon all hope ye that enter here."[17] If what is expected tomorrow looks no different than today, the future is perceived as bleak and uninviting, devoid of possibility.

If the future is meaningless, then activities such as growing, learning, and exploring seem like worthless endeavors. Furthermore, if the future is not to be trusted, then traveling forward toward it through searching and risking appears both foolish and dangerous. Hopeless people are in a threatening sea, holding on to a leaking life jacket called the present.

In this state of present-bound existence, a person assumes that this moment is all that exists; therefore, one must invest a great deal in the present. People who have been infected by hopelessness may have to distort the reality of the present to pretend it is something other than it is, because the "now" is their only chance for meaning. When the future is irrelevant, or not to be trusted, a person is abandoned to the present tense.

Enmeshment in a Finite Future Story

Finite hopes, as we said earlier, are not enough. When separated from transfinite hope, they leave us short of the fullness of our humanity. The danger with finite hopes is that they will be elevated to ultimate hopes. That is, a person will invest her or his total hoping process into finite content, which is unable to serve as an ultimate hope. Instead of keeping the finite hope connected to or in the context of ultimate hope in the character of God, a person can allow a finite hope to claim the status of ultimate hope. Earning the blessing of a parent, getting pregnant, finding a better job, or wanting the chemotherapy to be effective—these are appropriate goals in which a Christian could invest. However, when the hope invested in these goals is disconnected from a transfinite hope, then the finite goal or object must take on the heavy burden of being *the* future story—an ultimate concern. That is, the finite hope takes the form of a sacred story, but without God as the central character.

Finite goals, objects, and processes, of course, are not up to the task of being ultimate hope. They cannot serve as an adequate sacred story.

In theological language the content of that false hope is placed in the center of one's hoping process, thereby becoming an idol. Idols, as observation of the human condition makes abundantly clear, are not up to the task of being transcendent—they cannot provide transfinite hope.

Pastoral care intervention must confront the inadequate hoping process. Pastoral care helps people see that their hoping process has chosen inadequate content and is leading them toward despair rather than toward the hope of an open-ended future. Pastoral care and counseling enables people to recognize that they are making themselves vulnerable to despair by the shape of their future stories or their excessive investment in finite content.

Facing the Void

At various times in life, people become aware of the existential questions that come with the human condition. Being finite means facing tough questions about (1) loneliness—our awareness of life's basic aloneness and our attempts to overcome the fact that we can never be fully known by other humans; (2) meaninglessness—facing the "why?" questions about life and facing the fact that meaning in existence is not obvious, but has to be created by us; and (3) death—knowing that we will die.

Facing these questions is sometimes called facing "the void," [18] the absence of meaning, the seeming absence of transcendence. We know that facing the void is more likely to happen in the face of pain, suffering, and evil. Events such as war, cancer, violence, injustice, and other absurdities may enable hopelessness to establish a landing zone in our lives. Seeing what havoc a disturbed person can cause with an assault rifle, visiting the oncology ward at a children's hospital, walking through the museum at Dachau, hearing a trusted and loved spouse announce that she wants a divorce, attending the funeral of a doctor gunned down in his office—these are the life situations that raise questions about meaning and transfinite hope.

When people stare into the void, they may have one of two experiences. Some people encounter God. Christians believe that the Creator dwells even in this void. We may see in the void "the face of God," James Loder said, the transcendent source of hope in the face of the existential questions.[19] Others find the void filled with nothingness. They are not able to see the face of God. Many observers have talked about the loss of the sense of the transcendent, the suspicion that if a God exists, that God is not involved in day-to-day concerns of individuals. The feeling is that God either is not able to intervene or does not care enough to intervene.

Believing that God is present in the void, however, does not protect us from the anxiety we finite beings feel in the presence of the void. Things happen to us that make us face the void and raise questions about the existence of God, the character and power of God, and meaning in life. While our faith may restore our perception of God's presence, it does not keep us from seeing the void. Some people are faced constantly with the void and with the fact that their faith is not always strong enough to counteract the experience and provide hope for facing the void. Some Christians do not wait long enough for God's face to appear and are confronted with hopelessness.

We know of the close relationship between meaninglessness and hopelessness. When people claim that life is meaningless, they often mean that their life narrative has become unintelligible.[20] This can be perceived not simply as a loss of past roots or as isolation in the present (as crucial as these are) but as a loss of future story that makes sense. Their core narrative does not seem to be going anywhere. Everything has become relative and is, therefore, boring and without future.

When people see nothingness in the void they are threatened by hopelessness. Nothing is there, in what can they hope? It is a fearful experience. How do people respond to the threat? Many people have commented on the inadequate ways in which humans try to fight off meaninglessness, but few have talked about our ways of trying to deal with the hopelessness that is felt in the face of the existential questions. Hopelessness is all around us in ways that we hardly notice. Hopelessness hides itself behind and within certain lifestyles and makes itself invisible to those who do not have eyes to see and ears to hear.

Some people respond to hopelessness by choosing an idol. If they do not see the face of God in the void, they will create a god to put there. I call this the "Golden Calf Syndrome" after the experience of the Israelites in the wilderness. As described in the previous section, idolatry is the act of putting some finite person, thing, or idea in the center of existence in order to try to fill the transcendent void. A future story that has no transcendent reference is substituted for the sacred story that seemed devoured by the void. Then a person pretends that this sacred story is the source of hope.

Addiction is a primary example of idolatry. When we choose a substance (like drugs, alcohol, money, or food), or a relationship (with a spouse, parent, or child), or a function (like sex, religion, or work) to put in the center of life, this "thing" is given the place of a god in life. It becomes the center of attention (worship). It consumes our time, and we count on it to give us fulfillment. The pursuit of it dominates our time and energy. We are its servants. We are guilty of inappropriate bonding and identification. The "thing" becomes the ground of hope, which guarantees that we are set up for despair when this "thing" cannot deliver.

Negative God-Images

The character of the God in whom people believe and the nature of the experience they consider themselves to have had with this God determines whether religious belief promotes hope or despair. Without trying to establish when God-images begin or how they develop, we can say for our purpose that the character of these God-images affects the nature of hoping.

A person who develops a God-image filled with judgment and accusation feels less worthy than someone who has a God-image characterized by love and care. Those who feel that God is out to teach them a lesson, keeps a record of their sinful actions, and accuses and condemns them will feel despairing. When people feel that God is upset with them, they find it difficult to be hopeful. Their God is related to law rather than grace. The hope that was potentially theirs has been short-circuited by what they have learned about the nature and character of this God and how this God relates to humans.

Those who believe God loves them are more likely to think God calls them into a positive future, while the reverse is true of those who are not sure God even likes them and may be convinced, in fact, that their future will be filled with punishment or abandonment. Their faith does not give them a sense of hope, but actually leads to despair.

When God is not trustworthy it is difficult to have hope because not only is the finite future unpredictable but also any infinite future is under the direction of an angry, vengeful, disinterested, out-of-control, and ambivalent God. Such a God is not predictable. These God-images do not make it exciting to imagine being in the presence of this God. These people may have a future, but not a future to anticipate with hope.

Case Study: Debbie's Despairing God Story

Debbie, a young woman with a history of drug and alcohol abuse, came to a pastoral counselor because of her sense of being confused, trapped, and vulnerable. Concern about the future was primary. She had been in recovery through Alcoholics Anonymous for several years and was grateful for the help that organization provided. At present, however, she had dropped out of AA and was living with a man who used drugs and alcohol recreationally. We join the conversation with the counselor and Debbie:

DEBBIE: I feel like I'm living a double life, and sometimes I just feel like I wasn't that happy when I was doing it all the AA way. And I never found anyone I was happy with in AA. But then I'm not happy the other way [abusing drugs and alcohol]. You know, it's like I want to find a happy medium. It's one part of me wanting to give in to [her boyfriend's] side. It's kind of like good and evil. It's like evil's pulling me and good's wanting me and I don't want either one of them. (*with intensity*) I don't want to be Saint Mary anymore!—which I used to want to be. If God can't accept me the way I am, then to hell with him 'cause I've been through a hell of a lot and I'm never going to be Saint Mary! And yes, I'm still not married and I'm sleeping with somebody. I can't live up to the Bible and I can't live up to everything that is expected of me. And that's the way I feel and that's the first time I've ever been able to say that. You know?

P.C.: Good for you.

DEBBIE: You know—to hell with you, God! You're either going to take me or you're not. Where as before I've always been so damned scared of him that he's not even going to accept me or want me.

Debbie's story illustrates the contribution of a poor God-image to a despairing future story. Notice that the future story she wanted to give up includes a heretical God-image that added to her despair rather than bringing hope. The God she wanted to serve was perceived to be ambivalent toward her. She could not decide if she was acceptable to God. In fact, she wondered if God was "going to take me or . . . not," a reference to whether God would punish her severely for her sins, even taking her life. She had "always been so damned scared" of God, a response that does not, of course, produce much hope. Her works-righteousness theology ("I can't live up to the Bible and . . . everything that is expected of me") had failed miserably to provide a hope-filled life.

Pastoral Theological Reflection

Without hope, achieving life that has purpose and meaning is impossible. In fact, where there is no hope, sustaining human existence is difficult. "Without hope," says Royal Synwolt, "[humans] function at a level of existence which may produce illness or even death." [21] In *Man's Search for Meaning*, Viktor Frankl points out that many prisoners in the concentration camp died not from violence, disease, or hunger, but from giving up hope. [22] Erik Erikson's clinical experience convinced him that if a child does not develop hope, he or she will be emotionally stunted, deprived of the basis for healthy development, and will function at a lower level of maturation. Erikson summarizes, "Clinicians know that an adult who has lost all hope, regresses into as lifeless a state as a living organism can sustain." [23]

Many philosophers believe that hope can be grasped only in its relationship with despair. Tillich, for example, said, "it is understandable that all human life can be interpreted as a continuous attempt to avoid despair." [24] Marcel said, "I believe that it is only beginning from a reflection on despair and perhaps only from there that we can rise to a positive conception of hope ... hope can only be an active struggle against despair." [25] Marcel's metaphysic claims that hope is understandable only in the presence of the temptation to despair:

> We must declare very strongly that a philosophy which ... refuses to give a place to the temptation to despair, misunderstands in a very dangerous way a fundamental datum of our situation. In some way this temptation resides at the very centre of our condition. [26]

Notice that despair itself is not at the center of the human condition, but the temptation to despair. Marcel assumes that we have the freedom to choose against despair.

A continuing task of pastoral theology is to develop our understanding of despair. The psychological (maybe even biological), sociological, and spiritual factors that drain hope and make us vulnerable to despair call for our thoughtful attention. From clinical and theoretical perspectives we need to learn as much as possible about what Kierkegaard called this "sickness unto death."

6

The Dynamics of
Hope and Despair

The sense of hope is: there is a way out. The sense of hopelessness
is: there is no way out, no exit.

— William Lynch, *Images of Hope*

The relationship between future stories and hope and despair has been
described. Practical methodologies for making pastoral assessments and
interventions that nurture hope and confront despair are discussed in
chapter 7, but first I will explore three different characteristics of these
two human experiences. This chapter examines how hope and despair
are connected to reality, possibility, and community.

Hope and Reality

Hope is rooted in reality. Hopers relate to "what is" and have little
need to pretend. They are not afraid to face the "givens" of their past
and present (Kierkegaard's "actualities"), even while looking toward
that which calls us beyond "what is" into the future (Kierkegaard's
"possibilities"). People who hope do not need to dodge the facts or
obscure the objective data. Hope does *not* function as an opiate that
causes people to deny reality. In fact, hope provides the courage to face
whatever chaos and trauma life throws at us. Hope does not try to avoid
the pain of finite existence nor is it naïve about suffering.

Hopelessness, however, often attaches itself to unreality. People become vulnerable to despair to the degree they separate themselves
from reality by attaching their hoping process to fantasy and illusion
(such as in mental illness) rather than to reality. Superficially these fantasies resemble the dynamic nature and processes of functional hope.
In fact, as Lynch accuses, "they are a brilliant and exuberant counterfeit
of hope," and upon close examination we discover they are "the very
reverse of hope." These fantasies are dysfunctional future stories lead-

ing to false hope. In summary, to quote Lynch, "reality is healing for those who are without hope, and it is the separation from reality that causes despair."[1]

Stanley Hauerwas says of such fantasies, "When we do not understand we are afraid and we tell ourselves stories that protect ourselves from the unknown and the foreign." These are false stories that skew core narratives because they ignore reality. A true story, he says, is "one that helps me to uncover the true path."[2] True stories are rooted in reality and offer functional future stories that are full of hope.

Hopeless persons fantasize and distort reality because they do not have much confidence in the future. They deny reality because they think the future is not trustworthy or does not contain any solutions or possibilities. Their resulting hopelessness comes from not seeing "a way out." Since people must cling to some meaning structure of created reality, persons in dysfunctional circumstances are likely to create future stories that establish a false reality. Hopeless people must "see" what they think they can handle at the moment, since the present is all they have. If the here-and-now is all they feel connected with, they must shape their personal narratives to fit their wishes. Regardless of how destructive this "pretend reality" is, they feel better having a false reality than none at all. Hope based on distortions, however, turns out to be false hope that leads to hopelessness.

Reality and Reason

We must acknowledge the philosophical questions concerning the existence of reality, the content of reality, and whether humans can know objective reality. This is not the place for detailed philosophical analysis, but we can agree that reality as perceived by an individual is constructed from her or his unique intrapsychic, interpersonal, and cultural experiences. We know from our clinical practice that two people can have different perspectives of an event that both witnessed or of a relationship in which both participate. Pastoral caregivers must avoid stepping into the omniscient position of thinking that *we* know definitively what reality is in a given situation for a particular person.

Hope approaches knowledge about reality from a variety of epistemologies. Hope is related to a larger reality than that which can be ascertained by the scientific method and pure reason based on observable data. As soon as hope sets in, Paul Pruyser points out,

> the hoper begins to perceive reality as of larger scope than the one [he or she] has hitherto dealt with . . . and all knowledge becomes only a

knowledge of parts. But the summation of knowledges of parts does not yield the knowledge of the whole, which . . . thrusts toward novelty.[3]

We must respect this intuitive way of knowing if we are to understand all reality and not only that reality which is available through data and logic. Robert Carrigan points out that hope is imaginative rather than analytical because hope is more "intuitive, integrative, and wholistic" than it is "logical, analytical, or sequential consciousness."[4] Further-more, as Gabriel Marcel claims, the different aspects of hope are "be-yond the reach of all our faculties of reasoning or of conceptual formulation."[5]

In searching for truth about existence, hope does not make the mis-take of thinking that what we see and experience as reality is all the truth that exists. Since truth is embedded in temporality, it will be ex-panding and changing as the future approaches. "To the hoping per-son," says Carrigan, "reality is not fixed and crystallized; it is fluid and has resources that are as yet undiscovered and untapped."[6] Hopers know that truth, like time, is open-ended—there is more to come. Hope, therefore, accepts that there is mystery within reality.

Pastoral Theological Reflection

We dare to believe that God is ultimate reality, not ultimate fantasy. God relates to the reality of the created order, and so must we. A well-known passage from John's Gospel quotes Jesus as saying, "you will know the truth, and the truth will make you free" (John 8:32). Certainly the truth described here by Jesus has to do with reality as experienced with all our humanness: mind, heart, body, and spirit.

Mary Louise Bringle has suggested that a key event in the Christian story which speaks to the despairing person is the crucifixion.[7] In that "chapter" of the Christian sacred story, God embraced suffering as a reality of human existence. On the cross, rejection, loneliness, anguish, failure, pain, betrayal, and dashed dreams are all taken up by the suffer-ing God. Through the symbol of the cross, Christianity affirms that suf-fering is a reality within the human condition. When we face suffering, despair makes finite sense. But the cross reminds us of another reality within this sacred story, God with us. God is present with us in our deepest suffering, understanding and sharing our pain. We are re-minded by the cross that ultimately nothing "in all creation, will be able to separate us from the love of God in Christ Jesus our Lord" (Rom. 8:39).

Our sacred story includes the belief that God is present with us, suffering with us, saddened on our behalf, and working in mysterious ways to be known unto us. Part of reality and truth is that God's grace is already here, the kingdom of God is at hand, a new creation was brought into being through the Christ event. Therefore, an appropriate response to reality is to look for the signs of providence within the everyday happenings of our lives. These blessings can be found even in the midst of the traumas and tragedies that tempt us to despair.

Pastoral Care Perspectives

Pastoral caregiving affirms the reality of pain and suffering. We do not deny that life hurts. Whether we are ministering to persons who are negotiating some developmental stage (such as placing an aged parent in an alternative living situation), or dealing with long-term problems (such as alcoholism), or working on changing some aspect of self (such as a debilitating codependency), or facing an acute crisis (such as death and bereavement), one aspect of our care will be encouraging the parishioner to stay in touch with reality. We represent the reality of hope in the face of suffering. Because of hope, we can affirm and empathize with the pain.

When we offer care to a parishioner infected by hopelessness, part of our responsibility is to help this person locate reality. This reality includes a realistic grasp of her or his history and its influence on the present, plus realistic perceptions of present circumstances. Pastoral care helps people evaluate how the future stories within their core narratives are connected with reality. Hauerwas says that a true story must "demand that we be true and provide us with the skills to yank us out of our self-deceptions."[8] Functional hope does not result from chasing pipe dreams or absolutizing one portion of reality. The person must be enabled to face the reality of any given situation and challenged to start building revised future stories from that point. Staying in touch with reality means accepting one's freedom to make projections into the future and create one's own future stories. This concept leads to a discussion of possibility.

Hope and Possibility

Since hope is positively oriented toward the future while hopelessness views the future with suspicion, anxiety, or apathy, there are dynamic differences between hope and hopelessness in the way they affect thinking about "what comes next?" In the language of possibility, "hope is . . . a sense of the possible, . . . while hopelessness means to be ruled by the sense of the impossible."[9]

Hope is excited about the future because it perceives the future as open-ended, not determined but filled with possibilities. The reality present in the future is not predetermined but is "experience-in-formation."[10] Hoping does not limit reality to what is perceived in the "now" but continuously looks for further development of reality that is being formed. As the future unfolds, it reveals new data that change our understanding of reality. Reality for the hoping person is always in transition, fluid rather than static. Hope assumes the future contains potentialities not visible in the present.

Hopelessness approaches the future from one of four perspectives: (1) dread, fearing that the future will be a repetition of negatives from the past, (2) anxiety, assuming the future is dangerous, (3) suspicion, viewing the future as untrustworthy, or (4) apathy, assuming that the future will be meaningless.

Hopelessness views the future as closed and assumes change is impossible. Among the characteristics of hopelessness, according to Lynch, is the "sense of the impossible," the feeling that no matter what a person does, he or she ends up feeling checkmated.[11] This feeling is generated by the inability to imagine possible alternatives. W. W. Meissner, trained both as a priest and as a psychiatrist, elaborates:

> Hopelessness embraces a sense of futility, a sense of the unattainability of goals and purposes regardless of activity. What needs to be done seems to stand beyond one's capacity to perform or achieve. . . . [One's] perspective of the world and of [oneself] is immersed in impossibility.[12]

Hopelessness exists in a closed system, says Lynch, which operates on three assumptions: there are no "interior resources" for a human to call upon; there is no possibility for help from the outside; and, most devastating, even if interior resources existed and outside help were available, no sense or meaning can be constructed out of doing anything anyway![13]

Hope considers the potentiality that accompanies the future tense with wonder and is captivated by the as-yet-unseen options. Hope sees the present as pregnant, and it is curious about what might be birthed. Hopelessness, on the other hand, sees dead-ends, cul-de-sacs, and last chances. Hope is intrigued and fascinated by what is yet to happen, but hopelessness fixates on what cannot or will not happen. Hopers respond to the lure of the future, the pull of tomorrow. Hope dreams dreams! "Hope, therefore, is energized by belief in the possibility of getting somewhere, in the possibility of reaching goals,"[14] Lynch wrote. Hopelessness, however, is unimaginative and does not know how to dream.

Hopelessness also is characterized by what Lynch calls "entrapment," the opposite of freedom and possibility. "Hopelessness is rooted in structures of thought, feeling, and action that are rigid and inflexible. They are absolutized and repetitious structures that have become so many traps."[15] Hope, however, is adaptable and assumes that there are alternatives in any situation. If one option does not work, hope turns to another option with a sense of possibility. But hopelessness cannot find a way; nothing seems to work; it feels boxed in and stymied.

Hopelessness gets enslaved by repetitious patterns from a person's past. Fixation is the psychiatric concept that describes this aspect of hopelessness. This dynamic occurs when some wish, desire, need, or object becomes "absolutized," and a person places this concern at the center of her or his life. This person's range of thought, action, and feeling is narrowed. Imagination's freedom to visualize other possibilities and scenarios becomes severely inhibited and limited.

A classic meaning given to the concept of hope is that of transcending the difficulties and sufferings of the present, to look toward liberation from today's imprisonments. Hope looks for the proverbial "light at the end of the tunnel" and assumes a way out of the darkness that has descended on today. As Lynch says, "The sense of hope is: there is a way out." Hopelessness, however, expects no liberation, no moving beyond the present toward something new. Rather, "The sense of hopelessness is: there is no way out, no exit. It is the sense of impossibility, checkmate, eternal repetition."[16] Trusting the future and imagining possibilities enable a peaceful relationship to life, even when in crisis or battling with injustice. Thus a close relationship exists between hope and imagination.

Possibility and Imagination

With its expectation that the future will have options, hope can be imaginative about possibilities. Since imagination is able to envision the future, the possessor of imagination is not overwhelmed by the present moment. Hopelessness does not expect anything out of the future and, consequently, does not use imagination. A person with constricted imagination has difficulty being hopeful.

Hope is constantly imagining the unseen future and refuses to stop imagining, regardless of the situation. Imagination undergirds hope by continuously hypothesizing a way out, constructing new perspectives, and seeking a wider awareness of life and thought. Lynch calls the imagination "the gift that envisions what cannot yet be seen, the gift that constantly proposes to itself that the boundaries of the possible are wider than they seem." He describes this function thus:

> Imagination, if it is in prison and has tried every exit, does not panic or move into apathy but sits down to try to envision another way out. It is always slow to admit that all the facts are in, that all the doors have been tried, and that it is defeated. . . . [I]t is able to wait, to wait for a moment of vision which is not yet there, for a door that is not yet locked. It is not overcome by the absoluteness of the present moment.[17]

Only through the imagination can hope see a possibility for the future, conceptualize that possibility, and form it into a vision.

Hope is different from fantasy and illusion because it is related to reality. Because hope is realistic in its orientation, creative imagination is not out of touch with the present probabilities when considering future options. As Carrigan explains, hope "offers a new vision of reality that can be seen through faithful imagining."[18] The first task of this imagining, Lynch says,

> if it is to be healing, is to find a way through fantasy and lies into fact and existence. The second task . . . is to create perspectives for the facts it has found. . . . Like hope itself, it will always suppose that there is a fact and a possibility that is not yet in. The imagination will always be the enemy of the absolutizing instinct and the ally of hope.[19]

Lynch associates hope with the life of "realistic imagination," which is what he calls imagining that is in contact with reality. Satisfying future stories are those based in fact. To put it another way, reality is more productive of hopeful visions than unreality and produces functional future stories. Because of a lack of realistic imagination, those who are in crisis or suffering in some manner may depend on fantasy and illusion and end up with a dysfunctional hope.

Possibility and Risk

Hopeless people are frequently afraid of change. Though change is part of life's reality and cannot be prevented, hopeless people resist change. Hopers, however, try to manage change and participate in making it positive. Hopers trust the future and imagine possibilities, so they are not afraid to risk. A failure is not a disaster because it is not the end of potential. The future continuously supplies more possibilities. Concerning taking risks as a Christian, C.F.D. Moule says, we

> should daringly and at absolute risk cast ourselves trustfully into the deep which is God's character. To hug the shore is to cherish a disappointing hope; really to let myself go and to swim is to have discovered the buoyancy of hope.[20]

Hopers have a confidence that God "who began a good work among you will bring it to completion by the day of Christ Jesus" (Phil. 1:6).

Lack of trust in the future, plus an inhibited sense of what is possible, often expresses itself in obsessional, compulsive, or perfectionistic living. These lifestyles reveal a dependence on rituals to hold the untrustworthy or dreadful future at bay. The only security is perceived to be in preserving the status quo. To work with obsessional and/or compulsive people is to see the "trappedness" of hopelessness: they find it impossible to trust the future or open themselves to the risk of forgoing a compulsive ritual. When ministering to such a person, we must see the obsession or compulsiveness as not only a symptom of anxiety but a sign that hopelessness has established a toehold in this person's psyche. Pastoral intervention with such people must include confronting their idea of the closed future with the fact that they are not perceiving the possibilities in front of them.

Pastoral Theological Reflection

Death is the most formidable stone against which hope can be dashed. Christian theologians recognize the threat posed to hope by "the fact that every human being reaches an end when consciousness is extinguished, the life processes cease and the organism disintegrates."[21] When discussing Bloch's concept of "total hope," John Macquarrie points out its possible negation by "total threat," the threat of death in which "every human hope seems to wilt . . . [to] be cancelled out."[22] What is humankind to do against this monster of impossibility? Jean-Paul Sartre, a nontheist, was adamant that death "removes all meaning from life" because it destroys the context for fulfillment and meaning.[23] Does not death reduce all human hopes to rubble? Is not death the termination point for hope, the ultimate dead-end? The history of humankind includes hope that transcends death. Humans have always imagined, in a variety of contexts and visions, that existence extends beyond death.

Pastors and chaplains are constantly caring for people who are dying or facing life-threatening health problems—situations that often contain the seeds of despair in the face of "the last enemy." What do we represent with reference to possibility? Even in the face of the grim reaper the pastoral person represents the God of promises. We engage people as stewards of a tradition that proclaims possibility even in the face of the very real experience of death. The sacred story must confront death, because denying this reality is in the long run a hopeless stance. The Christian sacred story has as one of its core narratives the Easter story, the proclamation of resurrection. Those in this tradition are familiar with the idea that death is not the final word, even though the particulars of the sacred story's core narrative about death will differ depending on one's specific tradition.

From a narrative theology perspective, every person has a sacred story that includes his or her ultimate belief about the future. This story could focus on resurrection, immortality, immediate release into God's presence in heaven, lying dead in a grave until the Second Coming, living on in the memory of God, and so forth. Our responsibility is to enable persons to uncover these sacred stories about death and beyond, to help them find the resources in their own sacred story for facing death. When hearing a person's sacred story we must respect her or his language and symbols: the fullness of time, the second coming, the kingdom of God, eternal life, and even the pearly gates. If the story is forgotten, inadequate, or dissatisfying, we offer to remind, fill out, or change the story as communicated through ritual, scripture, and story-telling.

Pastoral Care Perspectives

Caring for persons who are feeling hopeless necessitates guiding them in the exercise of the imagination. Hoping is related to envisioning possibilities in both the present and future. If we did not have the capacity to fantasize, to picture in our "mind's eye" events that are "not yet," we could not hope. Since hope is future-oriented, we must be able to imagine ourselves and our environment being different.

Development of the imagination during childhood makes a significant contribution to the hoping process. Those who despair may not have had opportunity to develop their imaginations. In pastoral care and counseling, therefore, we take a stance that is intentional toward helping people open up their future by developing their imagination. We can help them expand their ability to imagine by asking them to draw pictures, read books about fantasy, go to the theater, or work with two-year-olds in the nursery at church.

One of our goals as caregivers is to help people suffering from hopelessness to change their assessment of the future. When despairing people imagine their immediate future, they frequently have only pessimistic, negative mental pictures. Often these future stories are dominated by the sense of helplessness. People communicate the presence of dead-end future stories with phrases such as: "That's impossible." "That will never work." "I can't do that." "I don't know where to go from here." "There is nothing else to do." Hopelessness has blinded them to the possibilities inherent in the situation. Our task is to help them deal with a life situation that appears impossible and the hopelessness that has entered their perceptual landscape. We can facilitate the development of alternative future stories.

Hope is always open to possibilities, so functional future stories are those which open up the future to the imagination. Hopeful future stories allow space for the potentiality inherent in creation to develop. Functional future stories are those that free a person to explore alternatives, to experience new things, to imagine change, to expect surprises, and to anticipate growth. Dysfunctional future stories are those that limit the future. Hopeless future stories serve to imprison the future of a person or system. When a person feels trapped by life, then future stories have lost the power to "open the way."

When people are unable to conceptualize stories for their future that "open the way ahead," we can confront them with the limitations placed on their hoping process. When people cannot activate their imagination we can ask why. We can ask, "How did you grow up without it? How did people respond to you when you pretended? What happened when you played make-believe? What occurred when you fantasized an imaginary playmate?"

When working with people who either cannot see or do not want to face the possibilities in their situation, we can point out the dynamic of hopelessness in future story language. "It is sad that this problem has closed down your future. It is as though a drape has been pulled, the curtains closed, the blinds turned shut on your future." The person can be challenged to resist the situation (or person) that is closing down her or his future: "This (problem or person) seems to be robbing you of the valuable gift of future hope. Can we prevent that from happening?"

The guidance function of pastoral care includes sharing possibilities. "Our lives change when new people open new worlds to us that transform the quality of our consciousness," John Navone said.[24] That is an excellent description of pastoral intervention. When a person's narrative is rooted in transfinite hope, he or she is empowered to choose and invest in finite hopes that give meaning to life. Pastoral care specialists have the privilege of either reminding people who are in crisis of their own sacred story or introducing them to a new understanding of the Christian sacred story, which can be the context in which future stories are transformed from despairing to hopeful.

Hope and Community

Hope is communal and relational, not isolationist and separatist. Clinical practice makes it quite clear that hope "does not exist in a vacuum, but rather in shared experiences with others," Robert Beavers and Florence Kaslow observed.[25] People who can hope are people who are meaningfully connected with other people. Marcel, too, believes hope occurs in relationships and doubts that hope can exist in an isolated individual. Joan Nowotny summarizes Marcel's position: "Completely isolated from any attachment to anybody or anything, [a person] has little reason to hope." [26]

Hopers have roots in some community with which they identify and with whom they feel bonded. Whether the community is their own family and friends, or a larger entity such as a nation or a church, hopers feel a connectedness with it. Belongingness is basic to hopefulness because, as Lynch says, "Hope cannot be achieved alone. It must in some way or other be an act of a community.[27]

Hope "is essentially a shared experience, hoping with or for others, which transcends the lone individual and his or her ego needs. Community is the vehicle of hoping." [28] Community becomes the context in which we learn to hope, so Christian community at its best produces hope. We look for community in which to share hope and share visions of the future. Hope pushes us toward relationships because it is trusting of others and thrives on intimacy and mutual love.

Hopelessness, however, tends to be suspicious of others and doubts whether other people can understand. Hopelessness pushes people into believing that they are not worthwhile, that people would be better off without them. When friends or family members withdraw or close themselves off from us, we need to consider the possibility that they have begun to feel hopeless. Since language is the economy of community, we can understand Marcel's words about the connection between "closed time," by which he means hopelessness, and "the rupture of all living communication with others." He demonstrates that

> to be enclosed in [despair] is by the same stroke to lose those spontaneous communications with other people which are the most precious things in life, which are even life itself. . . . In closed time friendship is no longer possible.[29]

"Perhaps it is impossible to really despair *with* someone," Lynch wrote. "Perhaps it must be a private act." [30] In this sense, the self closes itself off from other selves as it moves into despair.

Intimate relationships have the capacity to produce hope. An example of hope is found in the response of people who have "fallen in love." The excitement of the relationship opens up the future and produces energizing hope. Discovering a good friend can do the same thing: "When friendship is born, time begins to move again, and simultaneously hope awakens like a melody which stirs in the depths of memory," Marcel said.[31] The reverse is also true: relationships that fall apart may contribute to a loss of hope. Grief over the loss of some important person often leads to a sense of hopelessness.

Hopelessness and despair are more likely to exist in isolation. People infected by hopelessness are less likely to have meaningful relationships or a significant community. They do not feel deeply connected with anyone and are frequently without commitments to anything or anybody outside themselves. They tend to be isolated, alone, separated, disconnected, lonely, estranged, and/or alienated. Cure for hopelessness must include the discovery of relationship with individuals and communities.

Relationships that produce and maintain hope are characterized by mutuality of respect and care. In mutual relationships each person is helping the other to gain interior freedom, to achieve individual identity, and to become fully autonomous within the connectedness of the relationship.[32] Some relationships are destructive to hope, particularly relationships in which one person dominates, abuses, uses, or discounts the other. These nonmutual relationships make love conditional on obedience, submission, or dependence. The conditionality tends to make people feel trapped and stunts the process of individual growth and the development of hope. Terminating nonmutual relationships may be necessary because they foster despair rather than hope.

Hope and Trust

Hope is strongly related to the development of trust in early childhood. Erik Erikson concludes that those who develop the capacity to trust are most likely to feel and act hopefully.[33] He taught us that the most important psychosocial task of the first eighteen months is the struggle between trust and mistrust. Those who become more trusting than mistrusting usually have a more highly developed capacity to hope. Those who are more suspicious and doubtful find it harder to be hopeful.

Children who have been nurtured lovingly (held, touched, cuddled, talked to) develop a sense of trust in the world, and later, as they become aware that this nurturing is done by another person (self-differentiation), they learn to be trusting of others. They also develop trust in themselves because they sense that they are acceptable and lovable. Such trust in others and self provides a head start on believing in a God who is present, cares for them, and is concerned about what happens to them. They come to believe that the Creator is trustworthy and trusts them. This promotes trust and anticipation of what lies ahead, resulting in a hopeful perception of the future.

Those who do not receive care—who are not cuddled, touched, held, or talked to—tend to experience their environment as uncertain, unresponsive, and unpredictable. They are more likely to grow up suspicious about the world's trustworthiness and unsure that they are acceptable or lovable. They are likely to project this suspicion onto God and not expect God to be trustworthy or caring. Instead of developing positive expectations about the future that engender hope, they become vulnerable to an attitude of dread about the future which leads to despair.

Beavers and Kaslow believe that in the infant "hope is a biological given" that "can withstand much before faltering, overcome with cynicism and despair." They discuss how important relationships are to the development of hope by demonstrating that the clinical evidence makes clear that, on the one hand, "early loving and trustable interaction . . . contributes to enabling the child to cope with later disappointments, loneliness and loss." On the other hand, "the absence of emotional support and caring can produce a hopeless state." After reviewing the literature, Beavers and Kaslow conclude that despair is "created by unsatisfying, untrustworthy, confusing, cruel and/or depriving human interaction." [34]

Pastoral Theological Reflections

Mainstream theology has always conceptualized that God is personal, and that since we, as humans, have been created in God's image, we reflect that personhood. By describing God as personal, the Christian community conveys that God is relational, by nature a communal being. This intrinsic truth was captured by the Christian community in the doctrine of the Trinity—claiming that interaction occurs between Creator, Spirit, and Logos.

The Christian community has always believed that God's nature is characterized by the love called agape. What more basic theological phrase can be uttered than "God is love"! When Marcel gets to the foundations of hope, he discovers "the Thou who is the transcendent source and guarantee of absolute hope." [35] Nowotny describes it this way:

> The phenomenology of hope reveals an unconditional element at the heart of hope, a demand that love should have an absolute foundation. Since hope seeks its fulfillment in love, then hope also requires faith in

an absolute Thou who secures and confirms the communion of love. In
hope, love and faith are united.[36]

Since love, by its nature, must express itself in relationship, then
God must be not only a personal God but a relational God. Love does
not make sense unless there is a relationship in which this love can be
expressed and lived out. For Marcel, hope and love are close allies. As
he says,

> This means that in the first place hope is only possible on the level of *us*,
> or we might say of the *agape*, and that it does not exist on the level of the
> solitary ego, self-hypnotised and concentrating exclusively on individ-
> ual aims.[37]

Schubert Ogden says the love of God "is itself the object of Christian
hope as well as its ground."[38] Since hope is rooted in God's love, and
love implies relationship, then hope must happen in community,
whether between human beings or between human beings and God.
Hope for Marcel "involves a mutuality between persons and is ultimately a response to a Thou."[39] Hope is nurtured in relationship, hence
related of necessity to community, particularly the community of faith.

At its best, the church is extending community, particularly to those
who have minimum hope. The church provides a surrogate family that
accepts the hopeless into an intimate fellowship and cares for them in
ways that awaken hope. The church is a community of believers that is
both experiencing and expecting God's kingdom. This anticipation is
celebrated in the sacraments, which give shape to the present as well
as to the future.

Pastoral Care Perspectives

Given the foundational role that trust, relationships, and community
play in the development and maintenance of hope, what strategies can
the pastoral caregiver use in helping people generate hope and fight
despair? He or she can offer a trustworthy relationship out of which
hope can be born. Such a relationship begins with careful listening,
because recovering a sense of trust begins in the process of telling one's
story. Recovering hope, therefore, can begin by trusting another with
one's story of despair and feeling understood.

Karl Menninger has pointed out how important "hoping with" is to
patients and how much the medical and hospital staff help by their
hopeful attitudes.[40] The despairing person may have withdrawn from
others or been cut off from friends and family because of personal crises
with grief, depression, divorce, or unemployment. The pastoral caregiver "hopes with" suffering persons and allows these persons to "bor-

row" hope. A metaphor used by Royal Synwolt expresses this well: "The hopeful encounter becomes the stone quarry" from which despairing persons "find materials to build life anew." [41]

One goal of the pastoral relationship, therefore, is to guide persons infected with hopelessness in developing meaningful relationships with a community of hopers. The pastor represents God and the whole history of the Christian tradition—an identifiable community that projects itself into the future. Since hoping is a shared experience, it has a contagious quality. People can "catch" the atmosphere of hoping from the pastoral caregiver and the people of God with whom they get involved.

Part 2

Future Stories in Pastoral Care and Counseling

7

Hearing the Future Story

A part of the professional competence of a pastoral counselor is
to provide the creative kind of relationship in which innovations,
inventions, and the discovery of new alternatives is a daily event.
In short, this creativity engenders *hope*.
　　　　　　　　　　—Wayne E. Oates, *Protestant Pastoral Counseling*

Future has been identified as the primary dimension of time-
consciousness in which the struggle between hope and despair plays
itself out during the human pilgrimage. Within the future that is coming toward us we find possibilities and potentialities for our journey.
The visions, callings, and commitments that give our lives meaning and
fill us with hope are connected to our images of the future. Likewise,
within future stories the "temptation to despair" is most dangerous. To
nurture hope and combat despair, therefore, effective pastoral care and
counseling must attend to the future stories that humans produce about
this dimension of temporality.

The pastoral theology of hope developed in chapters 1 through 6
expands the methods and strategies of any level of pastoral care and
counseling—whether crisis intervention, supportive pastoral care,
short-term pastoral counseling, or more extensive pastoral psychotherapy. Now we turn to practical implications for making assessments,
attending to resistance, identifying dysfunctional future stories, deconstructing these dysfunctional future stories, and reframing and constructing hopeful future stories. Before proceeding with methodology,
however, I want to discuss the significance of pastoral conversation.

Linguistic Systems Theory

The process of exploring, confronting, and constructing future stories can be informed by the concepts of linguistic systems theory.[1] An
outgrowth of social constructivist thought, linguistic systems theory
holds that human beings make meaning through the process of commu-

nication. Rather than assuming that social systems create language and symbols, this theory claims the reverse, that language and communication create the social system. Linguistic systems theory posits that the process of constructing reality is conducted by humans "through the dynamic social process of dialogue and conversation."[2] We construct the realities that shape our existence through what Theodore Sarbin calls the "narratory principle" (see chapter 2). Narrative structuring, of course, occurs in the context of interactive communication and language. The process of relating to other persons creates the stories and core narratives that give substance to our identities.

What does this mean for assessing and revisioning the future and enabling persons to find hope? Since a person's dysfunctional future stories have been created out of the "world of conversational narrative," then change and growth must also occur in the context of conversation. We have established that the vehicle for narrative construction is language, so the methodology that will be central in the reconstruction of future stories will be the pastoral conversation—by which I mean conversation that is intentionally directed by the pastoral caregiver (at any level of pastoral care and counseling) so that professional skill can be focused on the tasks of healing, guiding, sustaining, reconciling, and liberating.

The pastoral conversation provides a safe environment in which a person or family can evaluate current future stories, generate visions of new potentialities, "try on" these possibilities, and savor the transformation. Changing the content of future stories during a pastoral intervention is primarily the task of language.[3] Language describes the possibilities that have been overlooked. Since language served as the vehicle for construction, it must also be the mode of deconstruction (see chapter 9).

Hans-Georg Gadamer taught us that no spoken word is complete or finished.[4] Every communication between human beings is filled with unspoken meanings, ideas, and concepts that are not yet clear. We have spoken of the future tense as the arena for possibility, and Gadamer's concepts remind us that every communication has possibilities for new interpretations that can be pursued. "Thus, the subject and content of all dialogue and discourse is open to evolutionary change in meaning," Harlene Anderson and Harold Goolishian wrote.[5] When a person's future stories are either dysfunctional or nonexistent, intervention through pastoral conversation facilitates that person's search for the possibilities that are buried in the "unsaid" of their core narratives. Anderson and Goolishian elaborate:

> Therapy relies on the infinite resources of the "not-yet-said" in the narrative around which we organize ourselves. . . . [Our] capacity for change is

in the ability we have "to be in language" with each other and, in language, always to develop new themes, new narratives, and new stories. . . . Change requires communicative action, dialogue, and discourse.[6]

Michael White and David Epston have emphasized narrative approaches to marriage and family counseling based on a social construction model. Since families have shaped their present narratives through language, they say, then therapeutic intervention should help the family "restory" their life situation in such a way that the problem is solved.[7] When we take seriously the constructionist viewpoint, we realize that a person or a family has the potential (freedom in the present, according to Kierkegaard's understanding of the self) to reconstruct the future dimensions of the core narrative.

Pastoral Assessment and Future Stories

Returning to the root metaphor of narrative, I want to assume that a primary task of pastoral caregivers is to be "listeners to and interpreters of stories," as Charles Gerkin says. He believes that people seek out a pastor or respond to pastoral initiative,

> because they need someone to listen to their story. Most often the story is tangled; it involves themes, plots, and counterplots. The story itself is, of course, an interpretation of experience. To seek counseling usually means that the interpretation has become painful, the emotions evoked by the interpretation powerful and conflicted. The search is for a listener who is an expert at interpretation, one who can make sense out of what has threatened to become senseless, one whose interpretation of the story can reduce the pain and make the powerful feelings more manageable. . . . [T]he one seeking counseling comes asking for a fresh interpretation of what has been experienced, a new "story" for his or her life.[8]

To be faithful as interpreters of life narratives we must know as completely as possible the stories that people bring to us.

Pastoral care and counseling at its best is marked by "an attitude of wonder and empathic, inquisitive respect [that] deeply values the life experience of persons."[9] Caregiving includes an empathetic quest for understanding how an individual is experiencing life. Knowing the "inner world" of the other, as we have learned from Boisen, is necessary to effective pastoral care and counseling.[10] I agree with the existential psychotherapists who believe that "our own human existence too, in its most immediate, internal nuances, will reveal itself if we have ears to hear it."[11] Pastoral caregivers have learned to appreciate the uniqueness of each individual's story and the importance of hearing it without prejudice—even though our broader knowledge about the human condition informs both our listening and our interpreting.

The awareness that we cannot know another person until we know that person's story is not a new phenomenon. Depth psychology from the time of Sigmund Freud to the present understands the significance of learning a person's story for comprehending her or his present situation. Most practitioners call this process "taking a history," conveying the analytic emphasis on the person's past.

Accurate assessment is the first step in the process of facilitating healing. We must find out what is happening. How did the problem originate? What is the content and context of the person's woundedness? Ministers trained in pastoral care know how to listen actively to "hear the person's story." Since the social and behavioral sciences influence our assessment techniques, we learn to concentrate our search for causes on a person's past and/or present (see chapter 1). Normally, "hearing the story" carries the connotation of listening to and gathering data about what makes up a person's history (stories past) and the details of the situation or system the person is in today (stories present). Because pastoral care specialists are interested in hope and despair, we must intentionally expand what we mean by "hearing the story" to include learning what a person is projecting into the future (stories future). Ben Furman and Tapani Ahola describe the opportunities of talking about the future tense:

> The future is perhaps one of the most gratifying subjects for therapeutic conversations. It is a country which no one can own and which is therefore open to all possible ideas and imaginings. People have different ideas about what lies in the future, and they may disagree about what it should bring, but since people know deep down that no one can ultimately know what the future will bring, it is a wonderful place for constructive conversations.[12]

These future stories are the central arena in which the hoping process can be assessed and effective intervention conducted.

Remembering that human brokenness always has a future component, we must find ways to investigate issues in a person's future stories that could serve as clues to understanding the problem. Since future stories are central to the core narratives that people bring to us for interpretation, hearing the whole story means developing acuity in hearing future stories. We must listen carefully for what these stories convey about hope and/or despair because future stories, like stories past and present, have hidden meanings that are not obvious in the data. To understand the place of hope and despair in the everyday lives of the people to whom we offer care, we must develop assessment strategies that enable us to be as proficient in assessing the future tense as we are at assessing the past and the present.

Exploring Future Stories

We have tools, such as intake forms, that give us information about past and present circumstances. We are well trained in taking personal, family, sexual, medical, and even religious histories. What strategies can we use to assess the future? What tools do we have that enable us to know what a person is thinking about her or his tomorrow?

Inviting Future Stories

During the initial phase of a pastoral intervention it is important to begin exploring a person's future stories, the shape of her or his hope. From the beginning we need to communicate our assumption that talking about the future and hope is as natural and as important to the healing process as talking about the past and present. Particularly in the context of a pastoral relationship, where spiritual issues are a natural, expected, and permitted topic, establishing the centrality of talking about the hoping process is not only appropriate but also an essential responsibility.

We invite people to tell us the "out there" as well as the "back there" and the "right now." We want them to tell us where they imagine they are going, what lies ahead, and what it is like out in front of them. We want to know what they are hoping for or dreading. This invitation takes a different shape, depending on the process of the pastoral interview and the context of the pastoral care event. For example, visiting the hospital room of a forty-eight-year-old dentist who has suffered a heart attack earlier in the day, talking to an eighty-three-year-old female resident of a retirement center two days after her husband died, and talking with an eleven-year-old boy whose parents told him the night before about their impending divorce, all require sensitivity to the future tense. When and how to bring the subject into any of these conversations, however, is more of an art than a science, so I cannot suggest any rules for the process.

In my own work, I try to find the earliest possible time to introduce the idea of future into the conversation in order to begin assessing how future stories are shaping and being shaped by the current situation. Either late in the initial interview, or in a subsequent session (depending on the process), I approach the subject something like this:

Thomas, you have told me about your personal history and about your present circumstances. However, I don't know much about what's ahead of you. Take some time and tell me some stories about your future.

The response may be one of surprise and uncertainty expressed in comments such as "What do you mean, stories about the future?" or "How can I tell stories about what hasn't happened yet?" If so, I take a minute to teach about temporality, explaining that everyone has images and ideas about the future that are central to the understanding of her or his life situation. Though still looking puzzled, most people launch into some attempt at describing their future. If they are not able to think of anything to say, they may ask: "What shall I think about?" or "How should I start?" or "What do you want me to say?" Then I ask them to tell stories about something that they anticipate, something that they think will happen or wish would happen, or to describe their dreams related to vocation or family. The following are some possible openings:

What do you think life will be like for you in five years?
What do you anticipate if things do not change?
What will you do if . . . ?
What are you most worried about?
Tell me about your daydreams.

We can invite people to tell us future stories about family members, other significant people in their lives, or institutions to which they belong.

Tracking and Expanding Future Stories

As people tell stories about their future, we can ask them to expand and elaborate in the same ways we pursue stories about their past and present. They often give only a brief outline of past events or present circumstances, and the caregiver must ask for more information in order to fill out the story. The same is true of future stories. The pastoral caregiver, therefore, can invite elaboration and ask for specifics:

Tell me more about . . .
Suppose that . . .
Where does your husband (wife, father, etc.) fit into that picture?
What will your health be like?
How would that be different if . . . ?

Have you considered how your future will change when (your mother dies, you graduate, the baby comes, etc.)?

Therapeutic goals for inviting and exploring future stories during the assessment process include: (1) to experience how persons project themselves into the future, (2) to identify the specific content of their future stories, (3) to assess the connection between their future stories and their present circumstances, and (4) to discover whether their future stories are contributing to hopefulness or hopelessness. Later in the intervention process there will be more specific agendas for exploring future stories.

Hearing the Contextual Story

Hearing and understanding the future story of any individual or couple must include hearing the larger narrative in which it is immersed (see chapter 2). Awareness of the future dimension of the ethnic, gender, socioeconomic, geographic, political, and cultural narratives allows a more thorough understanding of a person's future stories.

One reason to invite spouse, children, parents, friends, and/or other members of the extended family into a pastoral care intervention is to gain their understanding of the larger narrative, *including the future stories* dimension. These friends and family members will have perceptions about the individual's future stories as they are lived out in the context of extended relationships among family, friends, and community.

Strategies for Exploring Future Stories

As we move through the process of a pastoral intervention, we continue to pay attention to the place of future in both the assessment and, as we shall see in later chapters, the healing process. Since future stories are so important in understanding a person's life and in bringing about wholeness, attending to future tense during the entire helping process is important. Using various methods and techniques, we invite, even challenge, people to make the future dimension of their lives explicit, to become conscious of that which they anticipate or dread. We encourage them to get curious about their future, inviting them to find the answers to some of their questions about themselves in their future stories. We enable them to uncover unconscious future stories and overcome the resistance to sharing others. Pastoral caregivers can teach people that healing depends on uncovering and examining their future stories in order to learn how those stories affect their present motivations, desires, and behavior. Most therapeutic strategies used to help people explore their past history and present circumstances can be modified to include their future projections. This same method enables people to construct future stories that are more hopeful.

Storytelling

The most basic strategy is to invite parishioners to tell stories about specific future events. The caregiver takes initiative to choose a problematic issue, projects that issue into a future event, and then asks the person to create a story around that event. The story created will include many projections of conscious and unconscious material. Storytelling uses the imagination to construct stories that give particularity to what was previously unspeakable.

Clara, a thirty-two-year-old, single church employee, was struggling with ambivalent feelings about her father. The presenting problem had been the extreme anxiety she experienced during her father's recent cardiovascular emergency, which she feared would be fatal. Though I probed in a variety of ways, she found it difficult to talk about her relationship with her father. Finally I asked, "What will it be like at your father's funeral?" She was taken aback by my request, thinking it to be somewhat morbid. I asked if she thought that someday her father would die. She reluctantly agreed that he would have to die sometime. Then I asked her to tell me a story about her father's funeral. She finally accepted the assignment, but only if she could have time to think about it.

When she returned the following week she had written notes about a future funeral for her father that included who would be there, who would not be, and what would be said. Most revealing was her description of the emotional responses of her mother and siblings and why they would have certain feelings. The story allowed us to pursue the ambivalence of the family's relationship with the father. Most important, of course, Clara was able to speak about her own feelings when telling this story.

Many people enjoy communicating deeper aspects of their future stories through writing. Writing can be a helpful way to tell stories. I often use homework assignments in therapy. An effective one is to ask persons to write stories about future events to be discussed during the next session. People who like to write will often use journaling as a way of expressing their thoughts about the future and about the place of hope and hopelessness in their lives. Journaling about their everyday experiences often turns up material that identifies or clarifies their future stories. In fact, I have sometimes asked people to temporarily limit their journaling to material related to our discussions of the future and of the presence of hope and/or hopelessness in their lives.

Guided Imagery

The process called guided imagery[13] takes advantage of the human capacity for imagination and the ability to project pictures in "the mind's eye." The usual procedure is to invite the person to close her or his eyes and establish a meditative posture and attitude. When the person is relaxed, the pastoral caregiver structures a particular mental picture that moves the person into the content to be explored.

The caregiver can help a person picture a future time frame, imagine a particular event or circumstance, and then fill out the picture with plot and characters. The resulting narrative will reveal that person's own future stories. An example is my asking Jean to tell a story about what it would be like to visit her parents with a new baby (chapter 3). Her story opened the door to the future stories that explained her intense anxiety over her miscarriages.

Some people enjoy expressing themselves through artwork, such as painting, sculpting, or drawing. Asking people, particularly children, to create images of their future using their favorite art form provides another means for sharing future stories.

"As If" Conversation

These conversations are a strategy for allowing people to consider various possibilities by imagining future scenarios to be "real" for the sake of "let's suppose" conversation. Frequently this technique is used when relating to people who are anxious because of the uncertainty of their future. They are facing a threatening diagnosis, bad news from an employer, or significant conflict with an adult child but fear even to think about the possibilities. "As if" conversation bypasses the uncertainty of the moment and assumes certain possibilities that "could" be true for the sake of wondering about how one's future story would take shape if certain events occurred. "As if" conversation allows consideration of potentially threatening events on the horizon. These tension-producing events can be talked about with less anxiety when they are only possibilities and not actualities, when they are discussed in a "let's suppose" context.

As with guided imagery, the caregiver thoroughly explains the process and invites the person to participate. Granted the freedom to say yes or no, those who say yes are willing to give themselves to the exercise. When I think such a strategy would be helpful, I will say to the person, "I have an idea that might help with the anxiety you are experiencing. I wonder if you would have an 'as if' conversation with me?"

The person will normally ask what I mean by "as if" conversations. I then describe how I will set up a pretend situation about the issue he or she faces and then conduct a conversation as if what we were pretending was in fact the reality. Usually the person is curious about such a process and willingly agrees to participate. Let me give a generic illustration:

> Let's suppose that the doctor comes in tomorrow and tells you that it will be necessary to perform the open-heart surgery. Now you and I will begin a conversation pretending that news is given. What will we talk about after you have heard that information?

I can go on to ask, What will be your response? How will it affect your faith? your future? your relationship with the family? In this manner we confront a future story while it is only a possibility. The person has an opportunity to explore responses in advance and discuss possible changes that could be made if in fact that future story occurred.

Dreams

If your theoretical orientation and training permit you to deal with dreams, then enlist persons in examining dreams for content (symbols, metaphors, visions) that they perceive is related to the future. Stephen Crites is ready "to revive the age-old theory of dreams as hieroglyphs of futurity: not of the predictable future, which is nothing but an extension of the past, but of the indeterminate futurity of imaginative projection."[14] Dreams often reveal basic hope/hopeless themes that can enrich a person's understanding of unconscious future stories.

Perhaps more important is to attend to daydreams. Ernst Bloch taught us the importance of daydreams as a dimension of human experience in which the hoping process is often near the surface.[15] He points out that though daydreaming is not studied in the same depth that night dreams are researched, daydreams are the stuff from which future reality is constructed. Indeed, therapists may spend time helping clients capture and explore night dreams for clues to their emotional health, yet leave daydreams unattended. Pastoral caregivers can ask people to comb their daydreams as they would their night dreams for issues, concerns, fantasies, and frames of reference that might throw light on their perceptions of future.

Free Association

A common technique in psychoanalytic therapy is free association, a simple process by which the therapist asks the patient to verbalize whatever is going through her or his mind without censoring the content. The assumption of the analyst is that fragments of material floating through the patient's "stream of consciousness" are indicative of the unconscious processes that need to be uncovered in order to conduct an effective analysis.

This strategy can be helpful to the pastoral counselor when a person is having difficulty conceptualizing future stories. After describing the importance of future projections for assessing the hoping process, the pastoral caregiver can ask the person simply to describe whatever comes to mind about the future:

> For a few minutes I would like for you to tell me any thoughts, feelings, wishes, hopes, fears, fantasies, and so forth that go through your mind about the future. Don't try to decide if the idea is important or not; simply put it on the table and decide later whether it has anything to teach us about your future stories.

Often the content of these free associations will reveal the future story that is most problematic, the one that is casting the despairing pall over a person's life narrative.

If a person has difficulty thinking about the future, the process of word association can facilitate free association about the future. Actually the way I use this technique around future stories could more realistically be called "event association." I say to people, "I am going to mention a phrase, or describe an event, and I want you to tell me what thoughts and feelings go through your mind." Then I choose several phrases that seem to fit the context, for example, "next Christmas," "your fortieth birthday," "empty nest," "your father is in the coronary care unit," or "your mother finds out." After uttering the phrase, I wait for the response. Then I choose one response that seems most revealing and facilitate expansion and development of the future story.

Delimiting Pastoral Conversation to Future Tense

At some point, when working with a person who is stuck in the past, or bound by the present, or having trouble exploring the future tense, I will suggest that for a specific time, the conversation be limited to the future. Usually I choose a segment of the session in process:

> Edna, when I ask you to talk about the future, we seem to end up talking about what has already happened or what is happening now instead of what is yet to happen. For the next twenty minutes, I would like to limit our conversation to the future tense. Would you agree to that condition?

The person will usually agree, and then I describe how I will protect the boundary we set: "If you switch to past or present situations I will hold up my hand to signal that we have abandoned the future tense." Then using free association or any of the aforementioned strategies, I pursue conversation about the future tense and interrupt with the signal if the person falls back into the past or present during that time.

At other times I reserve a whole session for the future tense, saying:

> During our next session I want us to do something different. I want us to focus on your future, not your past or the present. I want everything we talk about to make reference to what is ahead of you, not what is behind you. So you might want to be thinking about how you see your future.

At that next session I repeat the agenda, leading with questions that invite her or him to focus on the future. When people have trouble doing this, I can then make the point that they are dominated by hopelessness as indicated by the difficulty they have in looking toward the future.

The process of exploring future stories is in itself a hopeful exercise. Consistently I find that pushing into the future, opening that dimension of life to exploration, contributes positively to the hoping process. Even when the future stories we uncover are frightening, the act of making them speakable seems to energize pastoral conversation at any level from supportive pastoral care to pastoral psychotherapy. Making the future speakable, however, is difficult for some people, a problem addressed in the next chapter.

8

Resistance to Exploring Future Stories

Hope is for the soul what breathing is for the living organism.
Where hope is lacking the soul dries up and withers.
—Gabriel Marcel, *Homo Viator*

Exploring future stories in pastoral care and counseling relationships can be more difficult than exploring past and present stories. Since communicating future stories to another person is not a common practice, individuals may feel uncomfortable at first when asked to explore their future images. Some people do not have much imagination and do not consciously project their future. Others are "present bound" and stumble over any consideration of the future. Playful invitation and gentle prodding will usually enable these people to bring their future stories into the pastoral conversation.

Other people, for both conscious and unconscious reasons, find thinking and communicating about the future difficult. From a therapeutic point of view, as we shall see, some of these difficulties are rooted in the same dynamics that create resistance to sharing personal history. Other dynamics come into play because of the unique threats posed by the future dimension of time-consciousness.

Future stories, like past stories, can be unconscious. We are quite aware that we repress and suppress some events in our past because they were so threatening. Pressed into the unconscious, these experiences can play havoc with a person's current life patterns. A common component of insight-oriented therapy is the recovery of these painful past stories for objective examination under the light of present perspectives. Sometimes these experiences are relived and reframed, then accepted as part of one's reality and integrated into life.

Persons also repress and suppress future stories because future stories can be just as threatening as past events. When we project ourselves into the future, we can imagine stories that are painful, stories that contain images of abandonment, failure, grief, abuse, and death. These stories are filled with dread rather than excitement, despair rather than hope.

Some people cannot communicate verbally their future stories because they really have blocked them from conscious awareness. These people are not resistive, but unaware. They simply do not allow themselves consciously to think about or deal with these future stories that are painful or threatening to self. Bringing these unconscious future stories to conscious awareness may be necessary for growth and healing.

When asking a person to explore and describe future projections about a relationship or a coming event, it may become obvious that he or she feels inhibited, uncomfortable, or even resentful about the possibility of discussing the future. This resistance may be revealed in statements such as

> I never think about the future.
> I've always thought it was useless to think about tomorrow, so I just try to get through the day.
> The future is so unpredictable, no use worrying about it.
> I have no idea.
> Who knows? I can't figure it out.

Some people's response to our attempts at meaningful conversation may be closed and uncooperative. They may seem apathetic, cautious, or reluctant in their response. Or they may actively oppose, thwart, or sabotage the process by refusing to talk or by steering clear of any significant conversation. We often use the concept of "resistance" to explain these behaviors.

Clients are reluctant to share their deepest concerns before they have decided to trust the therapist. What we call resistance is frequently the response of a client to a therapeutic process that seems coercive, invasive, or even unjust.[1] Robert Beavers, for example, describes the resistance that arises when clients feel an imbalance of power between themselves and the therapist.[2] Our first response to a person's resistance to exploring future stories, therefore, should be to evaluate whether we are functioning therapeutically in a way that elicits resistance. Are we intrusive, manipulative, or authoritarian in the relationship? Are we insensitive to the level of trust that has been established? unsuccessful in involving the person in a mutual decision to pursue the issue at hand?

Let's assume for our purposes that the relationship is well established, marked by trust and mutuality, and that the process is not invasive or coercive, yet the person is still resistant. Now what? We must turn to deeper definitions and understandings of resistance. In psychoanalytically oriented theory and therapy, resistance refers to a psychic process, usually unconscious, by which persons ignore obvious realities about their life and selfhood; defend against the exploration of certain painful events in the past; deny the characterological, affective, and/or behavioral patterns expressed in the present; or refuse to try new behaviors.

This traditional description focuses on past and present stories, but people also have similar resistance to exploring their projections into the future as evidenced by (1) ignoring the existence of future stories or refusing to discuss their content, (2) defending against the obvious hopelessness in the content of these future stories, (3) denying the contributions of these future stories to a dysfunctional hoping process and the intrusion of despair, and (4) refusing to reframe them in ways that aid the hoping process. Much of this resistance is caused by the pain and threat generated by projections into the future. This concept of resistance helps us understand the dynamics present when persons are uncomfortable about exploring some aspect of their future narrative. Why would people feel uncomfortable about telling us about their future? Several reasons are described here.

Dreadful Future Stories

Future stories, like past and present stories, can be anxiety producing. Asking people to narrate stories about an accident, an abusive relationship, or some other trauma in their history can elicit an anxious response. They may resist telling the past story to protect against reexperiencing the pain and terror. Likewise, present stories about domestic violence, economic failure, or medical diagnoses can be frightening and spark anxiety in the telling. People may fear the intensity of emotion that may be generated if they allow certain stories past or present to be spoken. They may fear becoming emotional and "falling apart." Resistance is their way of keeping the negative experience and possible consequences at bay.

That future stories may also be frightening should come as no surprise. In Charles Dickens's *A Christmas Carol*, Scrooge is more frightened by the Ghost of Christmas Future than by the Ghosts of Christmas Past and Present. A person may have future stories that contain imagined situations ("What if she divorces me?") or real events ("What will I do when he dies?") that invoke images of pain, separation, grief, and death. For many, dread is the affective response to their perceived future stories. One way they can handle this sense of dread is to keep future stories at the periphery of their mind; hence they are hesitant to share them with a pastoral caregiver. Like resistance to dealing with past and present stories, resistance to exploring future stories is a person's way of protecting the self from painful emotion.

Case Study: Delores's Dread of Being Alone

Delores, forty-two, is in the midst of a separation initiated by her husband of ten years. She has been seeing a pastoral counselor for several months and seems stuck, unable to shake the despairing mood and unable to act in any creative manner. Suggesting that she explore future stories, the pastoral counselor asks,

> What about the Delores of the future? Do you have any sight of what her future might be?
>
> DELORES (*pause, and then with intensity*): I see this person alone! And it bothers me—it still bothers me! (*pause, and then quietly*) My friends see it like "look, you have a new chance to find somebody else."
>
> P.C.: But that's not how Delores sees it?
>
> DELORES: I don't know whether I want to find somebody else.
>
> P.C.: Are you talking about six months or five years down the road?
>
> DELORES (*with intensity*): I'm talking old age! I'm talking about this woman who is going to be sixty-five or seventy years old. . . . How will I feel about that [being alone], you know?! What will I do about that?! I've got to make long-range plans.

After this interchange there is a pause. The anxiety about this future story of loneliness is palpable for both client and counselor. The image of herself being so alone is a dreadful future story that frightens Delores. As a result, the pastoral counselor and Delores collude in moving the conversation back to the present story of her husband's filing for divorce. The divorce is painful, but not as anxiety-producing as the existential issues of aloneness in the future.

Secret Future Stories

We must realize that some future stories, like some past and present stories, are secrets. Frequently a pastor or a therapist, in the confidentiality of the professional relationship, has parishioners or clients who share past stories that contain a core secret. "I've never told this to anyone!" they whisper. Then they tell a painful story about an attempted suicide, an aborted pregnancy, sexual abuse, or some other painful event from their history. People also invite us into present stories that are unknown to the general public or even close friends: an abusive spouse, a problem with drugs or alcohol, an affair, impotence, or some other carefully guarded secret.

We should not be surprised that people also have secrets about their projected future. In fact, some of the darkest secrets lurk in the anticipated or dreaded future, not in the past or present. People are hesitant to share these future stories, wondering if we would laugh, or reject, or expose, or judge them if we learned a certain scenario they are planning, or an event they want to happen, or a relationship they fear.

Some future stories are kept secret because they fall short of the ideals we want to believe about ourselves and convey to others. Future stories contain subplots that extend both our realities and our ideals into the future. As we project ourselves into the future, we want to mature in certain ways and accomplish certain goals (write a popular song, be helpful to people, make an important contribution, parent in creative ways) that we consider part of our best self. At the same time some aspects of our real self (shadow self, narcissistic self) have future agendas (to gain power over, to be admired, to earn lots of money, to see an enemy brought down) that we do not admire in ourselves. Most people, of course, would rather the pastoral caregiver did not see these aspects of the projected future that do not match their ideals.

A future story may be hidden because of shame. One may think of shame only in its relationship with past and present images of self. When people project themselves into the future, however, they may feel shame about the content (actions, thoughts, feelings) of their future stories. They would feel exposed if their colleagues, children, or loved ones were to know these stories. Even caregivers, of course, have these future stories that they consider shameful and hide even from themselves.

Case Study: Steve's Death Wish

During a difficult engagement, Steve's fiancée developed health problems and was diagnosed with cancer. Despite a poor prognosis, her dependency and his fear of rejecting or abandoning her led to marriage, despite his better judgment. Though she was expected to die within a year and went through a number of medical emergencies, she survived. They have now been married nine years, with two children. The marriage never really solidified. Steve does not feel love from her, only a clinging dependence and latent hostility. His anger at the way she behaves and the way she relates to the children has killed what passion existed in the beginning.

Steve was referred by his pastor because of chronic depression and stress that was causing problems in his work and in his relationship with the children. We stumbled along in the process of therapy looking at past, present, and future—though he was very resistant to exploring the future. Finally, after I had pushed him during several sessions to conceptualize his future, Steve decided to share the following:

> STEVE: I've been thinking about your ideas about my future stories. You're right—I do have one—I've been lying to you about not having one. I didn't want to tell you—it's a real sore part of me.
>
> P.C.: Future stories can be quite painful.
>
> STEVE: I carry it around with me and worry that people might guess it. Sometimes it is all I have to help me through the day, but then I feel so guilty—it is a terrible burden!
>
> P.C.: Really heavy.
>
> STEVE: I think you've heard lots of stuff in your job, so I've decided to tell you and hope you won't think I'm too terrible. (*pause, and then quietly*) My future story starts with [wife's] death. (*pause, and then with anger*) I want her to die! (*pause*) I dream about what I am going to do with the insurance money [she had bought a sizable policy with her father's help as a young adult] and who I want to date. I can't believe I'm telling you this. (*pause, and then he blurts out*) I don't know why God doesn't strike me dead!

Wishing for someone's death is not unusual for people in unhappy situations, but Steve was embarrassed and ashamed to have such thoughts. They contradicted his Christian ideals and certainly were different from the perceptions of friends and family, who thought of him as the ideal husband caring for a seriously ill wife. Telling me at last this secret about his future hopes helped solidify our therapeutic relationship and get the process unstuck. He had lanced a swollen, infected part of his psyche that was related to the future rather than the past.

In situations like the one related above, the pastoral caregiver hears confessions about the future. Pastors often deal with guilt related to events in the past or present dimensions of a person's life. However, people often feel either shame or guilt about their future stories. They need to be accepted and forgiven for behaviors and attitudes expressed in their future projections, just as for behaviors and attitudes from their past or present. Mediating forgiveness is a ministry related not only to stories past and present but also to stories future.

When someone does share future secrets with us, it can provide a turning point in the helping process. We have all experienced the dynamic of having a person finally take the risk of telling us a deep secret about her or his past, which establishes a deeper level of trust and provides a breakthrough in the therapeutic process. This same dynamic can take place when people tell us secrets about their future.

But like secrets from the past, however, some future secrets can be revealed too soon. We should not push a person to reveal a future secret before he or she is ready. The pastoral or therapeutic relationship can be broken by a secret, past or future, revealed before its time. Once a woman told me too quickly a future story about her desire that the child she was carrying from forced intercourse with her abusive husband would abort so she could feel free to move out of the relationship. The revelation came too early (near the end of her first session), and shame overwhelmed her. Trust between us had not been established, and she felt overexposed. She refused even to make another appointment, saying she was too embarrassed and hoped she would never see me again.

Magical Thinking and Future Stories

A third reason for resistance to telling future stories is the fear of magical thinking. This term describes the cognitive process that leads persons to believe that their thoughts and actions can determine external events apart from the normal pattern of cause and effect. This phenomenon is a primary thought process common to children and primitive cultures and is symptomatic of some mental illnesses. Any adult, however, can fall into this pattern of behavior under certain duress, particularly when faced with circumstances that are threatening to the person's sense of self.

Putting images into speech grants a different reality to a thought or feeling. For many people, expressing an internal perception by the spoken word endows that thought or feeling with a life of its own. If the thought or feeling is threatening to the self, the act of speech can be perceived as a way of "tempting the fates," somehow causing something to happen that would not have happened if the idea had been left unspoken. Magical thinking also can lead to a belief that if a desire is put into speech the possibility of its fulfillment has been thwarted. The cultural taboo against revealing the wish one makes before blowing out the candles on a birthday cake is one example.

Case Study: Don't Tempt Fate

In a course on pastoral care in crises, I invite students to imagine their own death by filling out a blank copy of an official medical death certificate. Filling in the blanks forces them to choose not only a cause of death, but to identify place, date, time, process of dying, and surviving members of the family. This exercise provides an opportunity to focus attention, through imagery, on a future reality (namely one's death) by creating a future story.

This exercise always produces some degree of anxiety for each student and is quite revealing of magical thinking. Some students are too anxious to participate and refuse to imagine their death or fill out the form. Others choose the safest course by answering a future-tense question with a past-tense story. They select a "date of death" that predates the class period. This protects them from dealing with a future scenario by turning the exercise into a "past story" and avoiding the possibility of "tempting the fates." Still others push the date of death into the nonthreatening distant future by projecting a story in which they die peacefully in their sleep at ninety-five years of age. Notice that each of these options protects the student from having to risk projecting a date of death in the near future, which is in itself an example of magical thinking—the fear that they could trigger their own death by daring a prediction. Some students are willing to share a future story they actually have considered (suicide) or fear (dying with cancer or being murdered). A few students, however, will courageously take the risk of fantasizing a death that will occur in the near future, which can activate magical thinking and the resulting anxiety. The following story illustrates this fear.

One student filled out the blank death certificate by imagining his death to occur on the Friday afternoon following that class period. He described himself dying in an automobile accident at a particularly dangerous intersection he passed every weekend while returning to his home in a distant town. The following week, when I debriefed the class on their experiences after filling out the certificate, this student shared that, to his considerable surprise, he had been unable to make himself drive through that particular intersection on the previous Friday afternoon (which he had identified on his certificate as the day and time of his death). Though he felt totally irrational and foolish, he drove sixteen miles out of his way to avoid that intersection! That is magical thinking. Rather than "tempting the fates," people will resist putting some future stories into words and sharing them in pastoral conversation.

Resistance to Change

A therapeutic process that carefully explores a person's past tense and connects this history to present life circumstances normally produces a heightened awareness of self. People usually welcome this new level of self-awareness, this recovered knowledge about core narrative and identity. To gain insight, however, is to be confronted with the possibilities of life and the need for change. People are not always interested in change, as we know well. Change carries its own threat and may even feel dangerous. In therapy we see people struggle with the question of whether or not they want to be different. When they are not ready for change, they will be resistant to the ongoing therapeutic process.

Changed frames of reference about one's self also come from examining future stories. Insight gained into future stories may call for accepting responsibility for these future projections that the person is unwilling to consider. If a person is fearful of the changes that being responsible would demand, he or she will resist bringing these future stories into consciousness and/or resist putting them on the table with the pastoral caregiver. This fear is another reason for resistance to further self-awareness about future stories.

The Pastoral Care Specialist's
Painful Future Stories

If pastoral care specialists are to be effective in overcoming an individual's resistance to exploring the future tense, they must be aware of their own future stories that could cause counterresistance. Like blind spots created by painful life experiences in the past and/or present, pastoral care specialists who have dreadful or dysfunctional future stories may find it difficult to hear or respond to the future stories of others. They will steer pastoral conversations away from the future dimensions as a way of protecting self from the emotional pain engendered by their own future story.

Case Study: Joseph's Fear of Suffocation

Joseph, a twenty-seven-year-old minister, was referred to me by his clinical pastoral education supervisor in the third quarter of his internship. Joseph had been confronted about avoiding the oncology ward to which he was assigned. When he did begin pastoral conversations with these patients, it became clear in case presentations that he steered conversations away from the subject of dying. Finally he had confessed to peers his long-standing anxiety about death.

In therapy Joseph hesitantly discussed several frightful experiences with death that occurred in the funeral home owned by his parents. During childhood he had frequently dreamed about being suffocated by various assailants and death by natural phenomena. Related to these nightmares was the ongoing future story that had plagued him for years; namely, that he would die by drowning or being "buried alive." A second future story that had bothered Joseph had to do with fantasies that when death did occur, he would be in some isolated situation that would prevent his family from finding his body. Joseph had never fully discussed the past experiences that had shaped his fears, nor completely verbalized "in the light of day," as he called it, his future stories. They lost much of their power when brought to consciousness. In fact, he experienced so much relief that he was able to share his story appropriately with several oncology patients in ways that were quite facilitating.

In summary, people have understandable reasons for being resistant to bringing future stories to consciousness and/or sharing them with a pastoral caregiver. Obviously, since creatively resolving painful future stories in a therapeutic context is as important as resolving past and present stories, pastoral caregivers must patiently work with persons until they can face these painful future stories. Chapter 9 discusses how to confront dysfunctional future stories when they surface.

9
Confronting Dysfunctional Future Stories

It therefore becomes evident that a conversion or a social revolution that actually transforms consciousness requires a traumatic change in a [person's] story.
—Stephen Crites, "The Narrative Quality of Experience"

A pastoral theology of hope, I have argued, is based on an anthropological reality: humans make sense of the future dimension of time-consciousness by constructing future stories about the possibilities coming toward them from the future. These future stories are a primary ingredient in a person's core narratives. Furthermore, we have established that disturbances of these future stories can lead to, or result from, human brokenness. When future stories are lost, disturbed, or distorted, then human beings become vulnerable to hopelessness.

Functional future stories are those future projections of our core narratives that open up life and invite us into an exciting, meaningful tomorrow. They are "hope-full" future stories that answer the "What happens next?" question by providing meaning and values that enrich life and make us want to persevere. Functional future stories complete our life narrative with "plot endings" that are satisfying and energizing, inviting us to trust that continuing to live is worthwhile. They provide the "get up and go" of daily living.

The hoping process becomes disturbed and vulnerable to despair when a person's future stories become *dysfunctional*. The term *dysfunctional* has entered our assessment vocabulary to describe families and institutions that are significantly hampered in their ability to fulfill their purposes. Dysfunctional future stories are those that cannot fulfill the purpose of future stories, to provide reasons to keep on moving into the future with hope.

We have seen that narratives are teleological, that they are headed in some direction (chapter 2). Mary and Kenneth Gergen describe how the movement of life narratives can proceed according to only three forms: (1) *progressive*, which means positive movement toward valued ends (an exciting engagement moving toward the wedding), (2) *regressive*, which means movement toward negative goals (a disintegrating marriage headed toward divorce), and (3) *stable*, which refers to narratives that move forward but are neither progressive nor regressive (a routine marriage).[1] Functional future stories maintain basically a progressive form. That is, we perceive our lives to be headed in directions that are satisfying. Dysfunctional future stories, of course, are primarily regressive, accomplishing the opposite of functional future stories. They lead to despair, not to hope. When a person's hoping process gets attached to a dysfunctional future story, then he or she becomes vulnerable to despair.

Change and Transformation

When a pastoral caregiver is involved with a person or family in crisis, some change or transformation in future stories is necessary for a satisfactory resolution and the recovery of hope. I have demonstrated that past and present time grounds us by setting limits, but future time, as Søren Kierkegaard taught us, provides the context for change. Pastoral caregivers represent two realities: (1) as we learned from Heraclitus long ago, we cannot step into the same river twice—change is inevitable and the future keeps coming toward us whether we like it or not, and (2) human beings have the freedom and responsibility to influence what shape the future will take. We try to guide people to accept their freedom, as Kierkegaard called it, in the now to affect the not-yet, to create new future stories.

What enables (makes, allows, causes, prompts, invites) people to change? How can a therapist or pastoral caregiver facilitate this change? These are formidable questions in the behavioral science literature. One helpful answer that fits the perspective of pastoral care and counseling is for the caregiver to become involved in the frame of reference of the person in crisis. In marriage and family therapy this is called "joining the system."[2] The therapist enters the world of the clients and becomes part of the system in order to change the system from within by adding new perspectives and interpretations. Many theorists suggest this joining or entering the system is what initiates change—doing so is a powerful agent of transformation.

From a Christian perspective the incarnation was a pivotal intervention: God became flesh and dwelt among us. God entered and joined the human dilemma through the work of Jesus the Christ, effecting change both in the historical context of his ministry and in the eschatalogically based, ongoing mission of the church.[3] The future is exciting because it is the place where potentiality lives. The pastoral theology of hope we have shaped declares that the future dimension of temporality is the arena of change and possibility. Scripture attends to change under such concepts as deliverance, redemption, salvation, and reconciliation—becoming a new creation or a new being. As pastoral caregivers we have the privilege of representing a community that is committed to hope and change.

Researchers describe two basic types of change: first- and second-order change.[4] First-order change refers to a change that occurs within a frame of reference or a worldview that already exists. Second-order change is more intensive, challenging the basic premise of the existing frame of reference or worldview. First-order change modifies or reshapes the content of an existing worldview, which causes a change of direction. In contrast, second-order change disrupts, even destroys, the current construction of reality, calling for a completely new frame of reference.

The root metaphor of narrative describes how selfhood is created out of uniquely personal interpretations of life events (stories) that form core narratives that shape personal identity. Using narrative theory, and focusing on the future dimension of temporality, we know that change occurs only when a person's stories are restructured. That is, if change is to occur in a person's life situation, or sense of self, or expression of that selfhood, then some transformation must take place in that person's core narratives. A new construction of future possibilities is necessary. First-order change affects several aspects of a future story, but does not change the entire core narrative. Specific content within the core narrative is modified but the larger frame of reference does not change. Second-order change, however, challenges the validity of the core narrative. The entire core narrative must be restructured. Most of the change required in the core narratives represented in our case studies was second-order change. The functionality of the whole narrative must be called into question. Before discussing the construction of hopeful future stories (in chapter 10), I must describe the deconstruction of dysfunctional future stories.

Deconstruction Theories

Effective pastoral care and counseling includes reclaiming, revising, rehabilitating, and reframing dysfunctional future stories. When faced with dysfunctional future stories hindering the hoping process, we must clear space for the creation of hopeful future stories by guiding persons in dismantling their dysfunctional future stories. This necessity is described concisely by Crites:

It therefore becomes evident that a conversion or a social revolution that actually transforms consciousness requires a traumatic change in a [person's] story. The stories within which a [person] has awakened to consciousness must be undermined, and in the identification of [her or his] personal story through a new story both the drama of [her or his] experience and [her or his] style of action must be reoriented.[5]

We will use the concept "deconstruction" to define the process by which such "undermining" is accomplished. Though the word *deconstruction* has a long history in philosophy, we will use this concept as it has been adopted by literary criticism and by psychotherapy.

In literary criticism, the term *deconstruction* describes the process of dissecting a text into its component parts for analysis. When the literature under review is fiction, then the deconstruction process "examines the ways in which plot, character, time, situation and authorial perspective articulate building a story."[6] When the literature is presented as faction (material presented as truth based on fact), then the deconstruction process examines the narrative to see if it is self-validating, exploring its basis in reality and evaluating the truthfulness of its interpretations. Using narrative theory as a guide, I suggest that the stories of a person's life are the phenomenological equivalent of narrative literature, "oral literature," if you will. But what is the genre of our future stories? Are they fiction or faction?

Our answer must begin by asking about the content that forms future stories. What material is projected? Some of the projected content is based on actual data from the history of that person and/or from what is happening in that person's present situation. This content is composed of factual material from past and/or present that is projected into the future. Additional structure is contributed by the imagination as it interprets what the data from past and present might look like in the future. This framework for the content of a future story is more like fiction because it grows out of the unique hermeneutic applied to the not-yet of a person's narrative. Thus, future stories are a mixture of fiction and fact. Given this mix, the deconstruction process must examine and make assessments of future stories on criteria that have to do with both fact and fiction.

In psychotherapy, particularly as developed within the schools of family therapy and brief therapy, *deconstruction* describes the attempt of a therapist to change a client's perception of reality. The term refers specifically to the process by which a therapist searches for a hole in the logical construction of a client's frame of reference as applied to a particular life situation or aspect of existence. The therapist is looking for the inconsistencies in a client's worldview, or as Steve de Shazer said, "searching for some point, any point, in the client's logical system that is 'alogical,' a point that will bring down the whole of the problematic construction."[7] To deconstruct in therapy is to challenge the client's structure of reality, or as de Shazer describes the process, the therapist "seeks to find the element in the system . . . which is illogical, the thread . . . which will unravel it all, or the loose stone which will pull down the whole building."[8] This process is not unlike the use of parables in the New Testament. The parables told by Jesus represent a new reality that, if understood, forces the hearer to adopt a new worldview.

Where do we look for the inconsistencies, the illogical pieces that make the future story vulnerable to challenge? Taking temporality seriously means searching in both past and present stories to find clues that material projected into the future is misinterpreted. The content that makes a future story dysfunctional will have roots in both the past and present.

Deconstructing Dysfunctional Future Stories

Constructivist theory (see chapter 3) holds that human beings create their own reality and live with the consequences. The intrapsychic or interpersonal crisis represents a future story constructed with a framework that leads to dysfunction. Psychotherapy based on constructivist theory starts from the premise that a client's *perception*, or construction, of the problem *is* the problem. Therefore, reconstructing reality as viewed by the client is a way of solving many problems. Deconstruction is usually the first step in this process. Deconstruction can focus on either first- or second-order change. The confrontation can either focus on a single future story or challenge the whole frame of reference, the futurity of the core narrative itself.

Case Study: Leonard's Exposure Story

We begin by discussing a first-order deconstruction in which only a part of the core narrative is being challenged. Leonard had developed a future story in which homosexual behavior during his college days would be exposed and he would be rejected: divorced by his wife, alienated from his parents, and fired by his congregation (see chapter 3). All three images were within the realm of possibility, so how could the future story be challenged? Leonard explored the level of anxiety he perceived about each substory and decided that the threat of his wife's rejection carried the most potential pain. I asked Leonard how he could test the reality of this piece of his future story. He finally concluded that the only sure way was to tell his wife about this college experience. We discussed how he could approach such a conversation. Although it was an anxiety-provoking choice, it allowed him to face a dreadful future story and provided an opportunity to confront his larger fear. When he did share his previous experiences with his wife, she assured Leonard that though learning about his behavior during college made her anxious, her feelings for him would not change. In fact, she understood how a person could need to explore sexual identity, because one of her male friends at college had talked with her extensively about his similar struggle.

With this piece of his dysfunctional future story discarded, its power was reduced. After considering the other two substories, Leonard decided that telling his parents was not necessary. Given their difficulties in accepting his sister's divorce, he assumed that such a revelation would strain the relationship. Furthermore, Leonard and his wife talked over what they would do if this past story ever made it impossible for him to be a pastor. Together they constructed an optional future story about what he would do vocationally if that scenario ever unfolded. Developing an optional future story about an alternative career freed him from his fear of unemployment. In short, Leonard reconstructed future stories that supported the reality that he could survive the consequences of having this past story known by his wife, parents, and church.

One characteristic of dysfunctional future stories is that they represent an end-setting that limits or closes down the future. Leonard's future story pictured cataclysmic consequences and implied that he would not survive such a calamity. In reality, of course, he could survive, but his interpretive assumption had to be challenged. Developing the possibilities in another vocation provided an optional future story that offered an open-ended future, a characteristic of hopeful future stories.

Case Study: Jason's Heart Symptoms

Next we examine a dysfunctional future story that called for a second-order change. Jason (see chapter 3) was a man in his early forties who was referred by his physician because of ill-defined heart symptoms that seemed to have no physiological basis. In response to my question about future projections, Jason said despairingly, "There won't be many tomorrows." When I asked for elaboration, he described the early deaths of his father and grandfather due to heart problems and his belief that he, too, would die in his early forties. The first session ended with the following transaction.

PASTORAL COUNSELOR: It seems that you are carrying around a pretty heavy future story. What connections do you see between this future story and your concerns about health and depression?

JASON: I really hadn't thought about that.

P.C.: I have a hunch that there might be some connections, and I would like for us to explore those if we can get together next week. Would you take time to consider how this view of the future affects your day-to-day life, write down your findings, and discuss them with me?

Jason agreed to return and to carry out the assignment. At our next session he indicated that he had been more depressed than usual because normally, he tried "not to think about these things." When I asked about his assignment, Jason smiled and said this:

JASON: I guess when a man sits in front of you because of heart symptoms which the doctor can't find reasons for and then tells you his grandfather and father died with heart problems, you would think there was some obvious connection!

Now what? At this point I directly introduced the deconstruction process. Since future stories contain our projections of material from past and present stories, they are perceived (often at unconscious levels) as true because through our frame of reference, our constructed reality, this data seems factual. The deconstruction process includes examining the future story to assess whether it is based on all of the data available in one's past and present stories.

P.C.: The first thing we need to do is find out how realistic your future story is. But that calls for a pretty thorough examination of the story. Would you like to explore it?

JASON: I'm game.

The first step is to see that the future story is fully understood.

P.C.: Let me see if I have the future story clearly in mind. You believe that since your grandfather died of a stroke at forty-two and your father of heart trouble at forty-one, you will die for the same reasons in the next year or two. Is that accurate?

JASON: I've never said it out loud before, but you got it.

The second step in deconstruction is to learn thoroughly the content from which the future story was constructed.

P.C.: The first question to answer is why you have decided that because they died at the time they did and in the way they did that
you will follow suit.

JASON: Well that is obvious! I'm like them.

P.C.: Why and how did you decide you were like them?

JASON: My grandmother says I'm just like my father, and I know
I'm the spitting image of my dad. (*pause*) And I'm the next male
in line.

The third step in deconstruction is to uncover the relevant data that
could have been included in a particular future story. While collecting
the data, the therapist is looking for the gaps in a person's perception
of reality. The view of the social constructivist and the literary decon-
structionist overlap at this point. Robert Steele identifies five tools, or
criteria, used in the deconstruction of material that is presented as factual: Has the author/narrator (1) omitted any data? (2) interpreted the
data with consistency? (3) tailored any of the evidence? (4) depended
on "mythic accounts"? (5) reported with any unexamined biases of perspective?[9] Steele uses these criteria in evaluating the truth claims of
autobiography. Since future stories are part of a person's narrative autobiography, we will examine Jason's narrative using several of these criteria.

All five of Steele's questions call for a clear picture of the data from
which a person has constructed a future story. To assess the data a person is projecting into the future, the counselor must recover from a
person's past stories the material from which the person shaped the
future stories. We must lead the person to evaluate the validity of this
material and find what data have been distorted or left out of the construction of future stories.

P.C.: You seem to imply that you are a genetic copy of only those
two people. Tell me more about the rest of your family's health
history.

In the conversation that followed I carefully questioned Jason about his
family of origin in order to discover whether Jason was dealing with the
total story concerning his genetic inheritance. Sometimes, as in Jason's
case, the future story has been so suppressed that it remains largely unexamined.

When we completed this thorough history by constructing a geno-
gram, Jason could be challenged with the following data. His paternal
grandmother lived until she was eighty-seven years old, and one of his
grandfather's brothers and one sister out of four children lived into their

eighties. His father's two brothers and one sister were still alive and well, though one brother had had a mild heart attack four years earlier. Jason was reminded that he is also the recipient of genes from his mother's side of the family, where there were several deaths from cancer, but no early deaths from heart disease. Both of his maternal grandparents lived into their seventies and his mother was in good health at sixty-three.

Obviously Jason had omitted from his future story the health data on everyone but his father and grandfather, resulting in a future story with tailored evidence. In reality his total genetic history did not predestine him to an early death by heart attack, so the data had been inconsistently interpreted. I challenged Jason to enter into the database from which he was projecting his future story the fact that in his family's history were some strong cardiovascular genes.

We uncovered an interesting and significant past story that served as a primary contributor to his anxiety. He remembered as a young teenager overhearing his grandmother say to his mother, "Jason is so much like [grandfather] and [father], I just hope he doesn't have their heart!" At that age he made the assumption that since he was "just like them" he must "have their heart," which meant his heart was weak, vulnerable, and would give out early in life. Jason tailored the evidence for his future story to fit this powerful past story. He had created a future story that was biased by his perception of his grandmother's "prophecy," a mythic account of his heritage. Bringing this past story to consciousness and putting it on the table for examination was helpful in taking away some of its power over his future story.

Another part of the deconstruction process was our examination of differences in lifestyle between Jason and his predecessors. Jason was asked about risk factors for heart disease. Both his grandfather and his father smoked all their lives, but Jason only smoked briefly during high school and quit after his sophomore year in college. His father, who worked long hours as a store manager, rarely exercised except on the weekends and was slightly overweight. Jason was not in much better shape, but he did play softball frequently with a church team. Jason's wife, who did the cooking in the family, was knowledgeable about heart-healthy diets, so his diet was different from that of his father and grandfather. In short, Jason was invited by the conversation to face realities about risk factors that were in his favor but had not been considered in the construction of his future story. Jason was asked to evaluate whether he had omitted any important data, whether his future story was consistent with the data of his genetic history, and whether he had "tailored" any of the evidence. The obvious answers helped him bring into question the "truth" of his future story.

The therapeutic process of examining Jason's lifestyle also introduced the freedom issue. Jason was treating his future story as if he could not affect the picture he had projected. By our third session he was already discussing more changes he could make in diet, exercise, and weight control that could affect his health and longevity. He had started the process of reconstructing his future story.

Case Study: Jean Can't Have a Baby

Jean and Frank were grieving over their third miscarriage and trying to decide whether or not to try for a fourth pregnancy (see chapter 3). One of Jean's future stories was that she would "give over" her baby to her parents, who would accept the child and, therefore, give Jean a blessing that she had not received from them otherwise. How did we proceed with deconstruction of this future story? First, we checked this future projection for its relationship with reality.

> PASTORAL COUNSELOR: If I remember correctly, you have a sister with two children and a brother with one child, right?
>
> JEAN: That's right.
>
> P.C.: Describe how your parents have related to your sister and brother differently since they have had children.
>
> JEAN: Well, they don't enjoy having them around, really. They find fault with the way [the two siblings] live and the way they try to raise the children. [She went on to give specific examples of her parents' dissatisfaction with her siblings.]
>
> P.C.: So, thinking about it realistically, how would having a child affect the way your parents feel about you?
>
> JEAN: Probably not at all.
>
> P.C.: Then let's ask why you hang on to such an image.
>
> JEAN (*long sigh*): I don't know.

Bringing this awareness to the surface could be perceived as adding to Jean's grief and despair. But actually we facilitate hope when we help people deal with reality, because hope is based on reality (see chapter 6). Jean had been wishing, not hoping,[10] which became obvious to her when she compared her projected image to her real experience. Reality testing is an important ingredient in deconstructing dysfunctional future stories and helping people find hope. Deconstruction enabled her to grasp the difference between wishing and realistic hoping.

Furthermore, Jean's accurate perception that her husband wanted a child had somehow escalated into the idea that he could not be fulfilled in the marriage if he did not biologically father a child. She verbalized her deepest future fear, that he would leave her for a woman who could bear children. She had been emotionally abandoned by her father and physically abandoned by her first husband and, therefore, was tailoring the evidence on the basis of these past stories. She thought she could keep this husband from leaving by having children.

The data omitted was a realistic word from Frank. Since he was in the session too, Frank could give his response to her future story. He confirmed his interest in having children, but affirmed that the marriage commitment transcended the issue of whether or not to have children. She had absolutized his desire for children. She came to accept (as did he) his desire for a child and at the same time believe that his love for her and the marriage was more important than children. Now she had another piece of reality upon which to base a more hopeful future story.

We will return in chapter 10 to the construction of future stories that are more helpful.

Challenging Theological
Roots of Despair

From a pastoral theological perspective, pastoral assessment of future stories must include an evaluation of theological adequacy and validity (see chapter 5). Many future stories are dysfunctional because of poor theology and negative God-images. The deconstruction process, therefore, must include confrontation of either an explicit or implicit "theology of despair" and/or God-images that do not conform with the gospel. At one point in a session with Jean and Frank we had the following interaction (our relationship was one that allowed this type of "humorous but serious" conversation):

PASTORAL COUNSELOR: How does your theology, your understanding of your faith, inform your thoughts and feelings around this whole issue?

FRANK (*after they looked at each other for a moment*): I'm not sure. We really haven't talked about that very much.

P.C.: Could I share what our conversation reveals to this point?

FRANK (*with a smile*): Oh no, here it comes!

P.C.: Jean, I gather that you believe God loves those women who have children more than those who don't.

JEAN: No, I don't believe that!

P.C.: Oh? Well, I guess you believe that women who have children are better Christians.

JEAN: No, that isn't true either.

P.C.: Well, maybe you believe that women who have their own biological child have more to give to God.

JEAN: No (*chuckling*), you know I don't believe that!

P.C.: Well, you sure could have fooled me given what you have been
talking about the last few weeks. Why else would you feel so bad
about not having your own biological child?

JEAN: I guess we haven't thought about that for a while.

P.C.: You're functioning as if God's involvement with your lives
would come to an end if you could not have a child. Your hope
seems trapped in a little box labeled "biological parenthood." I
wonder if this limitation fits with your concepts of the faith? I
Surely the God you worship can call you into a future story that
does not include your own biological child.

We ended this session with an agreement that they would talk over and
write out their response to my question about how their faith influenced their response to the whole issue. Later, when evaluating the
therapeutic process, Jean and Frank identified this interaction as the
most crucial confrontation and the session that motivated them to re-
vise their future story about parenthood.

Confronting the
Contextual Narrative

Deconstructing a narrative must include enabling people to assess
the validity of the future stories present in the cultural context in which
their narrative has been constructed. As we have established, every person's narrative is enfolded within the narratives of family and of the
larger culture. Any narrative shares a worldview, a belief system, with
that of these larger systems. The fact that this belief system is shared
by others validates it in the eye of the narrator. Deconstructing a narrative is more difficult to the degree that the narrative is embedded in
the larger cultural worldview. Individuals will find it more threatening
when the pastoral care specialist is challenging a narrative that is so embedded.

The pastoral caregiver must be concerned with justice issues. Many
larger narratives contain elements destructive of individual future stories. Cultural narratives about race and gender, for example, often contain future stories that are extremely limiting. The full range of
possibilities for human existence is not included in the future stories
that are modeled for those who grow up in such cultural contexts. In
fact, the culture may actively discourage and even prohibit certain
members, by virtue of gender, color, age, or handicap, from pursuing

certain future stories. Pastoral caregivers must actively engage these cultural narratives, fighting to open up the future stories so that all persons have access to the full range of possibilities within their cultural setting. Pastoral caregivers cannot separate the deconstruction of dysfunctional future stories that are internal and private from the necessary deconstruction of stories that are enforced by the external culture.

10
Construction of Hopeful
Future Stories

Our lives change when new people open new worlds to us that
transform the quality of our consciousness.
                    —John Navone, *Toward a Theology of Story*

We proclaim the good news that God brought into existence a world
that is "on the way," in Gabriel Marcel's words. Creation is in process
toward an open-ended future. We represent the God who is both with
us and out in front of us calling us, inviting us, even challenging us, to
move into this future. As Jürgen Moltmann put it,

> God is the one who accompanies us and beckons us to set out. And it is
> God who, so to speak, waits for us around the next corner. . . . Even on
> the false paths we take in life God continually opens up surprisingly new
> possibilities to us.[1]

The living God does not beckon from behind us somewhere in history,
but is pulling us toward the horizons of promise and fulfillment. Those
hurting people with whom we sit are crying out for a new horizon of
hope. They need future stories that provide security, excitement, and
joy in the present moment. Pastoral caregivers enable despairing persons to gain the courage to lean into their future, to revision and reconstruct future stories that are connected to hope rather than despair.

Charles Gerkin points out that the primary function of "a hermeneutical interpretation," which means revising a core narrative, is "to open
a way ahead."[2] Also concerned about the role of narrative in directing
us toward the future is Stanley Hauerwas, an ethicist who discusses
criteria for judging the truth claims of a person's story. One of his major
criteria is the effectiveness of human narratives to lead into the future
dimension of a person's life. "I am suggesting that a true story must
be one that helps me to go on."[3] Gerkin's "open the way ahead" and

Hauerwas's "helps me to go on" are both evoking the power of narrative to move us into a hopeful future.

Revisioning the future has significant power to change the present. Reshaping the future by projecting the self in creative new stories is important to regaining hope. By developing hopeful images of the future, people can regain excitement, motivation, purpose, and the deep joy that enables them to transcend the tribulations of the present moment.

Reframing Future Stories

"Reframing" is a concept from neuro-linguistic programming[4] and family therapy theory.[5] Frames of reference are those internal structures for understanding reality constructed through the narrative structuring process. These internal structures are the mind-sets, structures of reality, belief systems, or cognitive maps (depending on one's theoretical roots) that a person constructs to provide guidelines for turning events into personal stories. Frames of reference are the core narratives that we use to put events in perspective and make sense out of life.

To *re*frame, then, is to reshape one's perceptions, to change the cognitive sets by which one interprets an event or a relationship. Reframing is the process of helping a person, family, or group to transform the way in which they conceptualize a life situation. In a study of problem formation and resolution, three constructivists, Watzlawick, Weakland, and Fisch, offer this description:

> [Reframing is] to change the conceptual and/or emotional setting or viewpoint in relation to which a situation is experienced and to place it in another frame which fits the "facts" of the same concrete situation equally well or even better, and thereby changes its entire meaning.[6]

The therapeutic process of reframing is often used, as I describe it in therapy, to help people "rearrange the furniture" and "change the decorations" that make up a "certain room" in their memory. That is, they are enabled to change their understanding of a past story. The reframing process also is used to aid people in developing a new perception of a current situation, a present story. And for our purposes the technique of reframing can be used to help people reshape their ideas about the future.

People may reveal to the pastoral caregiver future projections filled with thought patterns that are obviously making their hoping process unproductive. The pastoral caregiver can intervene by helping them envision a future that "rearranges the furnishings" in their projected vision. If this psychotherapeutic process changes even one future story, a person's entire core narrative can be transformed and hope restored.

Some future stories, however, need to be significantly revised with new ideas in order to be hopeful. The story may have some content intact after the deconstruction process but is in need of reconstruction.

Case Study: Jean and Frank Find Options

After Jean deconstructed her dysfunctional future stories about having her own biological child (see chapters 3 and 9), she and Frank reconstructed their entire core narrative about parenting. The change took place from within their faith perspective, and it illustrates how reconstructing future stories can occur within the context of the Christian sacred story. They decided that one story was neither adequate nor necessary. Their core narrative about having children was restructured into three future stories. They summarized these stories as follows:

> JEAN: We decided that having children does not change our relationship with God or how God feels about us. It was ridiculous what we were thinking, and we never realized it—so unbelievable! We know that we can leave it open. We can have children or not—either way is fine.
> FRANK: We are going to try one more time to get pregnant, with the doctor's support. If that doesn't work, we will forget that.
> JEAN: We are going to put the word out about our interest in adoption and see what we can find.

In summary, they now had three possible future stories: they could get pregnant, adopt, or not have children. Most important, they could live with any one of these possibilities. They were not translating their finite hope to have a child into an ultimate hope. Jean in particular renewed her understanding of transfinite hope, broadening her awareness of how she had elevated a finite hope to ultimate dimensions, making an idol of having her own biological child. Recommitting to their sacred story gave them the freedom to pursue finite hopes without attaching their ultimate worth, or personal identity, to these finite objectives.

Constructing Future Stories

Sometimes, however, pastoral caregivers counsel someone who has no future story to reframe. When the person with whom we are working seems to have no future story, and therefore a disembodied hope, then part of the pastoral care task, and privilege, is to help that person create a hopeful future story "from scratch." In this situation we are constructing a future story to take the place of one which has been lost or blocked.

Case Study: Jason's New Vision

Remember that deconstructing Jason's future story included reframing his perception of his family's medical history and lifestyle differences. Once he accepted a new reality about his physical history, he had to construct new future stories around the open-ended possibility that he could live into retirement and beyond. He formed a new core narrative that moved from premature death as a certainty to death as the final chapter of a normal life span. Then he was able to form future stories about using his pension, having time for his avocation of sailing, and enjoying his children as teenagers and young adults. His despair was replaced by hope.

Case Study: Adrian's Escape Story

Adolescents who are in major conflict with parents or depressed over their sense of "stuckness" because of school, peer relationships, or romantic interests can experience despair over not being a self and being present-bound. Working with their sense of hopelessness can be difficult. Often they feel that the future has closed down, and they have no energizing future story. They project a future that is an endless repetition of the present. One therapeutic strategy in this situation is the construction of future stories that show them "a way out."

Adrian is a sixteen-year-old male in major conflict with his parents. He is angry about the way they relate to him, feels misunderstood and unappreciated, and is discouraged that he cannot be the perfect child they seem to expect, at least by their definitions. His father, owner of a small business, expects Adrian to make perfect grades because he is bright and capable. Because Adrian had experimented with drugs, his parents are now suspicious of his behavior and have a difficult time "cutting him some slack." The mother was difficult to work with, and the father refused to get involved in therapy. Adrian grew increasingly frustrated and began to believe that nothing could change, and a sense of hopelessness set in. Constructing a future story served as his bridge from the current standoff to a situation in which he could recover personal freedom. In the middle of a session the following exchange occurred:

PASTORAL COUNSELOR: Adrian, you are sixteen, but I can't remember the date of your birthday.

ADRIAN: I will be seventeen on [gave birth date].

P.C.: Let's see, that is seven months away plus twelve more months until your eighteenth birthday. That means that in just nineteen months you will be eighteen years of age and a legal adult. What plans do you have?

ADRIAN: None really, except I wanted to go to college.

P.C.: Would you mind if we had a conversation about your eighteenth birthday?

ADRIAN: What do you mean?

P.C.: I would like to have a conversation about your eighteenth birthday and discuss what that will be like.

ADRIAN: I don't see what good that will do, but OK.

P.C.: Tell me what you think that particular birthday will be like. What will happen?

ADRIAN: Like what?

P.C.: What will you do?

ADRIAN: What do you mean?

P.C.: Well, for example, are you going to stay home or move out?

ADRIAN: Move out?

P.C.: Well, you hate being at home so much that I thought you might pack and leave that morning. After all, you will be a legal adult, and your parents can't call the police like they did last year [when he left for two days and slept in his car].

ADRIAN: I hadn't thought of that. (*pause*) But I won't be out of high school.

P.C.: It doesn't matter. In this state the day you turn eighteen you are a legal adult, and your parents have no control over what you do.

ADRIAN (*looking off into the distance with a small smile on his face*): It would be nice to get out of there.

P.C.: Where can you go?

ADRIAN: I guess I could move out.

P.C.: There are so many options. You could join a branch of the military, rent an apartment, gain admission at a college that would allow you to start in the summer term, or take a trip around the country.

ADRIAN: I never thought about that!

From this point Adrian built a future story focused on establishing his own place of residence on his eighteenth birthday. He spent time examining the paper to see what apartments cost, planning a budget, and asking his boss how he could expand his work hours. His despair began to lift as he imagined the freedom that could be available in a foreseeable time frame. The most important result of his new future story was that it allowed him to see his parents in a different light. Now that he could assess the present against the horizon of his eighteenth birthday, a time when they could not control him, he was more tolerant of them in the present.

Encountering an
Unconscious Future Story

One problem that can be encountered when helping a person build a future story is the presence of an unconscious dysfunctional future story. In this context the unconscious story can be to the construction process what the iceberg was to the Titanic. The person will be in distress and function in an unexpected manner, but for unknown reasons. The most obvious sign that an unconscious story has been hit is resistance to constructing or to actualizing a new future story. In these cases the two stories, the existing future story (though unconscious) and the future story being constructed are in conflict, a "clashing of horizons."[7] The unconscious future story has to be brought to light, thoroughly explored, and deconstructed before construction of a hopeful future story can continue.

Case Study: Pam's Self-Sabotage

Pam, a twenty-two-year-old single female and a high school graduate, was in the process of constructing a future story that includes attending college when she struck a dysfunctional, unconscious future story. Pam discovered the conflict after being confronted with her resistance to taking effective behavioral steps toward the future story she was envisioning. She sabotaged her application process on two occasions. She finally admitted her hesitancy and was willing to explore the reasons for her behavior. She discovered an unconscious future story rooted in her past that pictured her as an inadequate student who "will never amount to anything." This future story developed around (1) past messages from a stepmother who frequently called her "stupid," (2) several embarrassing occurrences in seventh grade, and (3) a recommendation from her high school advisor that on the basis of her record she would find college a difficult task and should either enter a technical school or find a job.

Once Pam uncovered this unconscious future story, she was able to deconstruct it by specifically evaluating her stepmother's ability to judge a person's intelligence and aptitude for college work, which Pam laughingly conceded was not very high. She recognized that the high school advisor's recommendation was based on the record that Pam had accumulated to that point, rather than on knowledge of her natural abilities. Finally, a psychologist at the local junior college conducted a series of intelligence tests and aptitude inventories and supported the idea that she had the innate capacity to do the work. With the unconscious story deconstructed, Pam proceeded with the construction of a future story. She graduated from college and was employed by a retail chain.

Methods for Envisioning a New Future

Whether reframing or constructing future stories, envisioning the future in creative new modes is a therapeutic necessity. Developing strategies and methods for facilitating the envisioning process with parishioners, patients, and clients is imperative.

Stories are going somewhere—they are answering the question, What happens next? Mary and Kenneth Gergen described one of the most essential features of the narratory principle as being the capacity of narrative "to generate directionality" and provide "a sense of movement or direction through time."[8] Narrative directionality has three options: progressive, regressive, and stable. At any point a core narrative may be dominated by any one of these options. At other points, particularly in a period of transition or crisis, a life narrative may contain several of these narrative options.

A "dialectic narrative" is one in which two conflicting narratives, for example a regressive and a progressive, arrive at a point of conflict.[9] Within a dialectic narrative is the possibility that transformation will occur from this clash of contradictory stories. One way the pastoral caregiver can facilitate change, therefore, is by enabling a person to develop a progressive (hopeful) future story that has the power to confront that person's regressive (despairing) future story. The following methodologies can facilitate the construction of progressive future stories.

Storytelling

Storytelling is one way of identifying future stories (see chapter 7). Narrative theory also demonstrates the power of stories for affecting the way in which a person constructs her or his worldview (see chapter 2). I frequently invite those with whom I work to imagine a future story that is good news, one that has them reaching positive values and expe-

riencing a joyful life. Numerous possibilities exist for inviting a person
to tell a progressive future story:

> If your life was made into a wonderful movie with a happy ending,
> tell me what that last part of the movie would look like.

> If you wrote me a letter in a few years and it was filled with good
> news about your life, what would the letter say?

> If I read a story in the newspaper about some wonderful thing that
> happens to you next year, what would it be?

After they tell such a story, of course, I can ask them to expand the
narrative with content and characters in such a way that they construct
a fairly detailed future story. This story can then serve as a basis for
choosing creative behaviors, actualizing realistic possibilities, and
adopting a more hopeful stance toward their future.

Richard Gardner's mutual storytelling technique can be useful in
helping adults form more hopeful future stories. Gardner, a child psychiatrist, invites children to tell stories for his "Make-Up-A-Story Tele-
vision Program," [10] informing them that he, too, will be telling stories.
He instructs them to make up a story that has a beginning, a middle,
and an ending—taking narrative theory and temporality seriously. At
the conclusion of the story he asks that they tell him the meaning of
the story. Gardner then decides what part of the child's story needs to
be challenged in order to provide an alternative frame of reference.
Using the same characters and story line, he then retells the story with
a different plot and outcome. Caregivers can use these guidelines for
retelling a person's story about the future, creating a challenging dialec-
tical narrative.

For those people who find it difficult to speak about the future or
seem to lack the insight or imagination to develop a hopeful future
story, the pastoral caregiver can use a variation on Gardner's storytelling
technique. The caregiver can create and tell a story about a fantasized
future for the person. Hearing narratives about one's self from a trusted
and respected counselor can influence the way a person reframes or
constructs future stories. Therefore, telling stories that envision the future beyond where a person's own imagination can take them is a powerful strategy. The story must be connected to reality, but it can be
filled with realistic possibilities that expand their horizons and offer
hope. I invite the person to critique the story. Most people become
engaged in the process when another person begins to construct alternative future stories for them.

If family members, friends, or significant others are present, they can
be asked to contribute to the development of this future story. If they

are not present, I request that the person share with a significant other the future story I have created and solicit response. When people do begin talking about possible future scenarios, it is amazing how much energy can be generated not only in the person but in the family.

Guided Imagery

Guided imagery can help people uncover their future stories (see chapter 7). This process also can be used in helping people reframe, reconstruct, or construct a future story. After leading a person into a meditative physical and mental posture, he or she can be asked to form a mental picture as the pastoral care specialist describes possibilities for the future. Then the person can be led through various fantasies that suggest creative new ways of seeing the future and providing ideas for alternative future stories.[11]

Most people find this process an acceptable way to project themselves into the future, and it leads easily into storytelling. Sometimes, however, people find this imaging process difficult. They may be unable to give the inner self permission to fantasize. Some will feel resistant because they perceive imagery as being childish or irrational, and they may respond more positively to an "as if" conversation, described below.

"As If" Conversation

This type of conversation bypasses the reality at hand and assumes certain things that "could" be true (see chapter 7). It can be a helpful way to explore future stories that are difficult to make speakable. "As if" conversations allow a person to focus on potentially threatening occurrences that are placed in a "let's suppose" context.

"As if" conversation can also be helpful in envisioning new future stories. This strategy allows the pastoral caregiver to disempower threatening realities by leading the person to create a future story on the basis of additional data, both factual and imaginative. After rehearsing an existing future story, the pastoral caregiver can guide a person in developing a revised story through asking questions about the "as if" possibilities. The person can then review her or his future projections, reframing the stories by adding new characters, bringing a different twist to the plot, and arriving at different interpretations of the meaning of the event.

Deleting the Problem

Hopelessness is often focused on a particular problem that appears impossible to solve and seems to block one's journey into the future. Opening up the future in such a situation can be accomplished by helping people resolve the problem. Many excellent methods for problem solving are known. A problem can also be solved by developing a future story without the problem and then evaluating how this story could be made operational.

If clients cannot find clues to a solution to their problems in the past or present, William O'Hanlon and Michele Weiner-Davis ask them to "envision a future without the problem and describe what that looks like." [12] The process of imagining the future without problems is itself a creative, though difficult, task. These authors use what they call "fast-forward questions" to pursue the client's future projections, and say that "once the client describes the future without the problem, [the client] has also described the solution." [13] Often people have not taken the time to construct consciously a future story that does not have the problem in it.

Ben Furman and Tapani Ahola have developed a process in which they ask clients to imagine a future time when their problems no longer exist.[14] Then these therapists lead a dialogue (much like the "as if" conversations described earlier) about that imaginary future time. They ask questions such as, How is your life these days? Discussion continues around statements such as "Tell me about your (work, marriage, parents, problems)." Their clients usually enjoy fantasizing about life without the problems, or stresses, or crises of the present. Clients describe in detail what this "good" life looks like. After a while the therapists broach the therapeutic question, "What made all these changes possible?" Clients frequently are able to describe what would have changed in themselves and in those with whom they relate that allowed the fantasized future to occur. Within the client's descriptions of what was different are the seeds of healing. Furman and Ahola relate cases in which the construction of such a future story was the beginning of the healing process.

Imagining a Miracle

The concept of miracle has a long history. Human beings have always fantasized having the power to bring about a major change in life by waving a wand, saying the magic word, or finding a bottle with a genie who would grant three wishes. Steve de Shazer and his group take advantage of this desire for therapeutic purposes. They use what they call the "miracle question" to spark fantasies about the future.[15] They ask clients to imagine that they wake up one morning and find that their main problem is gone:

Your husband no longer uses alcohol.
You and Susan are remarried.
Your depression has completely lifted.
You weigh only 130 pounds.
No more conflict exists between you and your mother.

Then the therapist asks the clients to discuss what life will be like now that the problem is gone. They track this new future story with questions that ask the client to fill in the details: How will life be different? How will (husband, child, parent, friend) be different? How will you (act, feel, use money) differently? Where will you live? What will you be doing? Finally they ask what would be necessary to maintain life as described in this problemless future story. After enabling the client to elaborate on these ideas, the therapist uses the answers to guide therapeutic interventions and give shape to revised future stories.

Furman and Ahola point out that these processes of fantasizing or imagining a miracle can be used to expand, or go beyond, a despairing future story. Even if a client is thinking about suicide, the therapist may raise the future issue by asking the client to imagine that after death, she or he is met at heaven's gate by an angel who announces a reprieve and sends the person back to earth with all her or his problems solved.[16] "What will life be like for you with all the problems solved and a chance to start over?" Then they work with those possibilities to begin to construct a future story that is more workable in the present.

Spiritual Revisioning

Sometimes a person has a future story that does not go far enough into the future. It only reaches as far as what seems achievable right now. We can use Ernst Bloch's concepts to heighten our awareness that hope must reach further into the future than what can be immediately predicted, further than we have the specifics to make happen. Bloch argued that human beings need to have a hope that imagines possibilities that are not possible now but may be possible in the future. Perhaps these are the "dreams" of the poets, but they are certainly possible for the person who has a sacred story. The Christian story posits a future that transcends not only present reality and next year's possibilities but even this life's limitations.

Any caregiver, regardless of theoretical and methodological commitments, should be interested in dealing with future stories simply because so much human suffering is rooted in this dimension of time-consciousness. Pastoral theologians and pastoral caregivers, however, are interested in the future dimension for an additional reason—this is where ultimate concern takes us into religious experience with hope and despair. Foundational to pastoral care and counseling is the theological arena, where the hoping process can move out of the finite and into the transfinite. One of our goals is to help persons gain insight into the transfinite hope provided by their sacred story. We can enable them to include the hopeful sacred story in their confrontations with the crises, tragedies, problems, and other life circumstances that they face from day to day.

The pastoral care specialist, therefore, will focus on the future dimensions of a presenting situation even if such focus is not necessary to make the presenting symptoms go away. Consider, for example, a case study presented by O'Hanlon and Weiner-Davis, two well-known theorists and therapists from the solution-oriented school.[17]

> Bonnie was a 55-year-old woman who called for an appointment because of panic attacks which occurred whenever her dear friend, aged 70, left town or was not available to her by phone.

The therapist states that she would not have asked about Bonnie's family history because theoretically, in the "brief therapy" school of thought, knowing about the client's past is not considered important to therapy. However, during the "small talk" that took place at the beginning of the session,

> Bonnie revealed that her father had died when she was a baby and her mother, to whom she was very close, had died about two years before the session. . . . She also added that her completely healthy son, age 25, died in a freak, work-related accident.

The therapist asked Bonnie what brought her to therapy. Bonnie described the panic attacks that she had had for the last five years but mentioned that "for the last year and a half I've been doing much better." Consistent with solution-oriented brief therapy, the therapist ignored the history of losses. She reported that "the remainder of the session was devoted to exploring what Bonnie was doing to make things 'much better.'" The therapist further summarized that Bonnie came for help because "her friend was concerned that Bonnie would not be able to take care of herself in the inevitable event of the friend's death. Bonnie admitted to being extremely fearful about this."

Staying within her theoretical framework, the therapist did not pursue conversation about this fear, but complimented Bonnie on "how well she was dealing with her bad feeling" and on "all the methods she had developed on her own to make herself feel better" and even stated that she "was extremely impressed that Bonnie was doing as well as she was under the circumstances." The therapist also reframed two ideas. First, she suggested to Bonnie "the bad feeling inside" could be "loneliness," not a panic reaction. Second, she pointed out that Bonnie was giving her seventy-year-old friend purpose in life "by helping her feel needed and wanted," challenging Bonnie's view that she was dependent and helpless in that relationship. Bonnie was given a homework assignment to "notice what she did to overcome the temptation to call her friend or give in to the bad feeling if it occurred." A second session was scheduled in two weeks.

At the second session Bonnie reported having had a good two weeks. In one instance she did begin to worry about her friend. She was able to keep that concern from becoming "a panic attack" and listed the creative ways in which she intervened with herself. When asked by the therapist what she thought accounted for the changes, Bonnie mentioned that she moved from feeling helpless to recognizing that she was helping her friend. Bonnie, who felt better, agreed that termination of the counseling was appropriate and, as the therapist reported, "said she felt like skipping and jumping out of the office, and she did just that!"

This case presentation is an excellent example of the "brief therapy," "problem-oriented," or "solution-oriented" perspective on therapeutic process. The therapist dealt with only the presenting issue and focused the therapeutic intervention on the positive ways in which Bonnie could solve this problem. This case also illustrates, however, the shortcomings of any therapeutic intervention that does not confront the future dimensions of the situation. Most pastoral counselors would not have overlooked the significant losses Bonnie reported at the beginning of her first session. A more careful pastoral assessment would have included an exploration of the multilayered grief to see how much was still unresolved, examining the abandonment issues and searching for other possible contributors to her panic attacks.

For our purpose we need to point out the significance of her future story, which was not addressed by the therapist. Bonnie evidently had a future story that included (1) the sudden and perhaps traumatic (given the specific history of her losses of mother and son) death of her seventy-year-old friend, (2) her inability to handle that death, and (3) the possibility that she might engage in some bizarre acting out or have a total collapse in response. Even with these brief images we can make several assessments. First, Bonnie's core narrative about the future is deeply influenced by the death of loved ones, the resulting separation anxiety, the fear of abandonment, and doubts about her ability to survive another major loss. Second, this future story is disconnected from any transfinite hope that could provide the backdrop of a future horizon wide enough to embrace death and provide Bonnie with sustaining grace, meaning, and purpose in the face of such a separation.

At the very least, given what we have established about the future dimensions of human existence, a therapist should have asked Bonnie to describe her future stories and enabled her to bring to consciousness with as much specificity as possible what she imagined was going to happen. She may have had some nightmares about losing her friend, and she probably had daydreams about it also. She may have worked hard to keep specifics out of her mind (suppression of future stories) and resisted speaking of concrete possibilities, but the therapist, using any of the techniques described above, could have gently insisted that she give particularity to her fears. By making them speakable, she could withdraw their power as a despairing future story.

The theological anthropology we have established reminds us that at any point in a person's history, he or she has future stories that are important to her or his identity and sense of self. The loss or disruption of these future stories in the past can be a major cause of problems in the present. This knowledge could guide the pastoral counselor in this circumstance to help Bonnie recognize and describe her previous griefs and the way each of those losses radically changed the future story with which she was living at that time.

At the point when she suffered those traumatic losses she had future stories that included father, mother, and son. At three critical junctures her future stories were seriously disturbed. What did those losses mean to her future stories? What did she do to rebuild a future story? Or did she? Maybe she had been limping through life since one of those losses being "present bound," with dysfunctional future stories. Perhaps she has been fighting despair since the sudden, traumatic death of her son. Perhaps the threat of losing her friend forced an unconscious future story into the open through her anxiety attacks, providing an opportunity for creative pastoral involvement in recovery of hope.

Imagine what the pastoral caregiver might find if Bonnie told her future story, explored it fully, and made conscious all the suppressed fears. Then suppose she related these now-conscious finite future stories to the sacred story of her religious tradition. Suppose she became aware that her future story had not been informed by her sacred story. Suppose she explored how that sacred story might change the content of her specific future stories about death and abandonment, which were causing so much anxiety.

From a pastoral theological viewpoint and, therefore, from a pastoral counseling perspective, helping Bonnie make life adjustments that enable her to ward off panic attacks is neither sufficient intervention nor total care. Since these deeper issues have not been addressed, Bonnie has missed an opportunity to grow in her faith. She has not developed a future story informed by the sacred story that could be sustaining when her friend actually dies and in the face of other crises that life will throw at her.

These are major differences between the solution-oriented approach, which is interested only in finding a solution for the presenting "problem," and pastoral care and counseling. The short term is important for pastoral intervention, of course, but the short term is not adequate for the theological context of pastoral work. Short-term hopes are acceptable, but without long-term hope (made possible by transfinite hope), they leave us vulnerable. Pastoral caregivers assume that within every human situation are faith issues that can be addressed. If we stretch pastoral anthropology to include future dimensions of temporality, then every problem or crisis raises questions about future story and the theological issue of hope. Furthermore, every crisis is an opportunity for a person to learn more about her or his faith perspective, including the potential for developing a deeper understanding of the sacred story. This possibility necessitates attending to future stories and the hoping process.

The sacred story represents a progressive narrative. It represents a God-Who-Is-Love, a God who attends to us with steadfast, faithful care and is trustworthy. When a pastoral caregiver introduces, interjects, or invites this sacred story into the pastoral conversation with a person whose narrative is regressive, a clash of narratives occurs. This progressive, hopeful sacred story has the power to overcome a dysfunctional, regressive story and bring transformation into a person's faith narrative. The future is opened and a person's horizons are expanded. The God who calls us into an open-ended future, who grants grace for the present moment and energy for the journey, is "discovered."

Paul's famous closing words in Corinthians establish the "big three" of the Christian religion: faith, hope, and love (1 Cor. 13:13). Scholars have gone to great lengths to define, describe, and research the meanings of faith and love. These two words receive more attention from the pulpit and in publications than the third member of the "big three," but hope is equally significant. After all, "faith is the assurance of things hoped for, the conviction of things not seen" (Heb. 11:1). Along with faith and love, hope stands at the heart of Christianity, foundational to religious experience and mature spirituality.

Notes

Introduction

1. "Healing, guiding, and sustaining" are from Seward Hiltner, *Preface to Pastoral Theology* (Nashville: Abingdon Press, 1958), 89–174. "Reconciling" is from William A. Clebsch and Charles R. Jaekle, *Pastoral Care in Historical Perspective* (Englewood Cliffs, N.J.: Prentice-Hall, 1964), 56–66. "Liberating" is an addition I have been making in my pastoral care courses for a number of years.

2. Wayne E. Oates and Andrew D. Lester, *Pastoral Care in Crucial Human Situations* (Valley Forge, Pa.: Judson Press, 1968), 18.

3. David O. Woodyard, *Beyond Cynicism: The Practice of Hope* (Philadelphia: Westminster Press, 1972), 15.

4. Robert L. Carrigan, "Where Has Hope Gone? Toward an Understanding of Hope in Pastoral Care," *Pastoral Psychology* 25, no. 1 (fall 1976): 39.

5. For an overview, see Walter H. Capps, "Mapping the Hope Movement," in *The Future of Hope*, ed. Walter H. Capps (Philadelphia: Fortress Press, 1970), 1–49.

6. Carrigan, "Where Has Hope Gone?" 40.

7. John Macquarrie, "Pilgrimage in Theology," *Epworth Review* 7, no. 1 (January 1980): 47–52.

8. Wolfhart Pannenberg, *Anthropology in Theological Perspective*, trans. Matthew J. O'Connell (Philadelphia: Westminster Press, 1985), 15.

9. Ibid., 21.

10. Ibid., 15.

11. Charles V. Gerkin, *The Living Human Document: Re-Visioning Pastoral Counseling in a Hermeneutical Mode* (Nashville: Abingdon Press, 1984), 39.

12. Ibid., 21. Gerkin says, "Pastoral psychotherapy in its methodology has come to rest its primary work of decision making and action on psychological and psychotherapeutic criteria." Gerkin reports his personal concern with "the absorption of pastoral counseling ministry into psychotherapy to the point of loss of the pastor's rootage in the Christian tradition and language," p. 20.

13. See Anton T. Boisen, *The Exploration of the Inner World: A Study of Mental Disorder and Religious Experience* (New York: Harper & Brothers, 1952).

14. Gerkin, *Living Human Document*, 21.

Chapter 1. The Power of Future
in Human Existence

1. Stephen D. Crites, "The Narrative Quality of Experience," *Journal of the American Academy of Religion* 39 (September 1971): 305.

2. Ibid.

3. For an excellent collection of discussions about time by significant philosophers from Plato to Whitehead, see Charles M. Sherover, *The Human Experience of Time: The Development of Its Philosophic Meaning* (New York: New York University Press, 1975).

4. The classic texts are Martin Heidegger's *Being and Time* (New York: Harper, 1962), sections 65–69, 81, and Jean-Paul Sartre's *Being and Nothingness: An Essay on Phenomenological Ontology*, trans. Hazel E. Barnes (New York: Philosophical Library, 1956), 107–70.

5. Augustine, *Confessions*, Book 11, chaps. 18 and 20.

6. Ibid., chap. 20.

7. John Macquarrie, *Existentialism* (Philadelphia: Westminster Press, 1972), 156.

8. John Macquarrie, *In Search of Humanity: A Theological and Philosophical Approach*, (New York: Crossroad Publishing Co., 1983), 43.

9. Crites, "The Narrative Quality of Experience," 302.

10. Ibid., 303.

11. Ibid., 302–3.

12. See Søren Kierkegaard, *Fear and Trembling/The Sickness unto Death*, trans. Walter Lowrie (Garden City, N.Y.: Doubleday & Co., 1954).

13. Mark C. Taylor, "Kierkegaard as a Theologian on Hope," *Union Seminary Quarterly Review* 28 (spring 1973): 226–27. I acknowledge my debt to Taylor's research and to his translations.

14. Kierkegaard, *Sickness unto Death*, 164.

15. Taylor, "Kierkegaard as a Theologian on Hope," 226–27.

16. Kurt K. Reinhardt, *The Existentialist Revolt: The Main Themes and Phases of Existentialism* (Milwaukee: Bruce Publishing Co., 1952), 238.

17. Errol E. Harris, *The Reality of Time* (Albany, N.Y.: State University of New York Press, 1988), 87–92.

18. Don P. McAdams, *The Stories We Live By: Personal Myths and The Making of the Self* (New York: William Morrow & Co., 1993), 39–65.

19. An inclusive translation of a quote from Ernst Bloch taken from Harry J. Cargas and Anne White, eds., *Death and Hope* (New York: Corpus Books, 1971), 62.

20. I discovered this quote from Paul Tillich while visiting the Paul Tillich Memorial Park in New Harmony, Indiana.

21. Terrence McNally, *Lips Together, Teeth Apart* (New York: Penguin Books, 1992).

22. Heidegger, *Being and Time*, 376.

23. Ibid., 378.

24. Sartre, *Being and Nothingness*, 129.

25. Irvin D. Yalom, *Existential Psychotherapy* (New York: Basic Books, 1980), 11.

26. See a summary of Bloch's thought in "Man as Possibility," in *The Future of Hope*, ed. Walter H. Capps (Philadelphia: Fortress Press, 1970), which originally appeared as "Der Mensch als Moglichkeit," *Neues Forum* (Vienna), Vol. XIII, nos. 140–41, 1965: 357–61, trans. Walter H. Capps; Ernst Bloch, *The Principle of Hope*, Vol. I, trans. Neville Plaice, Stephen Plaice, and Paul Knight (Cambridge, Mass.: MIT Press, 1986), 67, a three-volume summary of Bloch's philosophy, published in Germany from 1954 to 1959 and finally translated into English; and in Wayne Hudson's introduction to Bloch's "Theory-Praxis in the Long Run" found in *The Sources of Hope*, ed. Ross Fitzgerald (Rushcutters Bay, Australia: Pergamen Press, 1979), 145–53.

27. Richard H. Roberts, "An Introductory Reading of Ernst Bloch's *The Principle of Hope*," *Journal of Literature and Theology* 1, no. 1 (March 1987): 91–100.

28. Bloch, "Man as Possibility," 62.

29. Reinhardt, *Existentialist Revolt*, 238.

30. Robert Beavers and Florence Kaslow, "The Anatomy of Hope," *Journal of Marital and Family Therapy* 7, no. 2 (April 1981): 119.

31. Jürgen Moltmann, *Theology of Hope*, trans. James W. Leitch (New York: Harper & Row, 1975), 286.

32. Ibid., 286–87.

Chapter 2. Narrative Theory and Future Stories

1. Theodore R. Sarbin, "The Narrative as a Root Metaphor for Psychology," in *Narrative Psychology: The Storied Nature of Human Conduct*, ed. Theodore R. Sarbin (New York: Praeger Publishers, 1986), 4. Sarbin borrows the concept of "root metaphor" from Stephen Pepper, *World Hypotheses* (Berkeley, Calif.: University of California Press, 1942).

2. See essays in Sarbin's *Narrative Psychology;* McAdams, *Stories We Live By;* Michael M. White and David Epston, *Narrative Means to Therapeutic Ends* (New York: W. W. Norton & Co., 1990); and Donald P. Spence, *Narrative Truth and Historical Truth: Meaning and Interpretation in Psychoanalysis* (New York: W. W. Norton & Co., 1982).

3. Alan Culpepper, *Anatomy of the Fourth Gospel: A Study in Literary Design* (Philadelphia: Fortress Press, 1983).

4. See, for example, James W. McClendon, Jr., *Biography as Theology* (Nashville: Abingdon Press, 1974). See also John Navone, *Toward a Theology of Story* (Slough, England: St. Paul Publications, 1977); Wesley A. Kort, *Narrative Elements and Religious Meaning* (Philadelphia: Fortress Press, 1975); Michael Goldberg, *Theology and Narrative: A Critical Introduction* (Nashville: Abingdon Press, 1982); George Stroup, *The Promise of Narrative Theology: Recovering the Gospel in the Church* (Atlanta: John Knox Press, 1981); and Stanley Hauerwas and L. Gregory Jones, eds., *Why Narrative? Readings in Narrative Theology* (Grand Rapids: William B. Eerdmans Publishing Co., 1989).

5. Sarbin, *Narrative Psychology*, 9.

6. Ibid., 8.

7. Crites, "Narrative Quality of Experience," 291.

8. Stanley Hauerwas, "Story and Theology," *Religion and Life* (autumn 1976): 343.

9. Kenneth J. Gergen and Mary M. Gergen, "Narrative Form and the Construction of Psychological Science," in Sarbin, *Narrative Psychology*, 25.

10. Mary M. Gergen and Kenneth J. Gergen, "The Social Construction of Narrative Accounts," in *Historical Social Psychology*, ed. Kenneth J. Gergen and Mary M. Gergen (Hillsdale, N.J.: Lawrence Erlbaum Associates, 1984), 173.

11. Alasdair MacIntyre, *After Virtue: A Study in Moral Theory*, 2d ed. (Notre Dame: University of Notre Dame Press, 1984), 205–14.

12. Ibid., 208. Narrative theorists believe human action is understandable only when attention is given to subjective issues such as motivations, purposes, values, and beliefs that transcend individual actions.

13. Jerome Bruner, *Acts of Meaning* (Cambridge, Mass.: Harvard University Press, 1990).

14. MacIntyre, *After Virtue*, 209.

15. Hauerwas, "Story and Theology," 344.

16. See the essays in Sarbin, *Narrative Psychology*, and the research documented in McAdams, *Stories We Live By*, 39–65.

17. McAdams, *Stories We Live By*, 39–47.

18. Crites, "Narrative Quality of Experience," 291.

19. Stephen Crites, "Storytime: Recollecting the Past and Projecting the Future," in Sarbin, *Narrative Psychology*, 159–60.

20. Gergen and Gergen, "Social Construction of Narrative Accounts," 174–75.

21. Crites, "Narrative Quality of Experience," 29. See Stroup, *Promise of Narrative Theology*, 101–18.

22. Hannah Arendt, *The Human Condition* (Garden City, N.Y.: Doubleday & Co., 1958), 181.

23. For a brief history of constructivism, see Ernst von Glasersfeld, "An Introduction to Radical Constructivism," in *The Invented Reality*, ed. Paul Watzlawick (New York: W. W. Norton & Co., 1984), 17–40.

24. See Gregory Bateson, *Steps to an Ecology of Mind* (New York: Ballantine Books, 1972).

25. For a well-known introduction to the neurological limitations on our perception, and therefore our construction of reality, see Heinz von Foerster, "On Constructing a Reality," in Watzlawick, *Invented Reality*, 41–61.

26. Bebe Speed, "How Really Real Is Real?" *Family Process* 23: 511–20. Also see Speed's "Reality Exists, OK? An Argument against Constructivism and Social Constructionism," *Journal of Family Therapy* 13, no. 4 (1991): 395–410.

27. Speed, "Reality Exists, OK?" 401–8.

28. Paul Ricoeur, *Time and Narrative*, vol. 1, trans. Kathleen McLaughlin and David Pellauer (Chicago: University of Chicago Press, 1984), 3.

29. Crites, "Storytime," 159–60, 165–75.

30. Ricoeur, *Time and Narrative*, 1:3.

31. Sarbin, *Narrative Psychology*, 3.

32. Crites, "Storytime," 155.

33. Kenneth J. Gergen and Mary M. Gergen, "Narratives of the Self," in *Studies in Social Identity*, ed. K. Scheibe and Theodore Sarbin (New York: Praeger Publishers, 1983), 255.

34. Sarbin, *Narrative Psychology*, 3.

35. Crites, "Storytime," 162–63.

36. Ibid., 159.

37. Ibid., 162.

38. See Spence, *Narrative Truth and Historical Truth*.

39. See Hauerwas, "Story and Theology," and Ricoeur, *Time and Narrative*, vol. 1.

40. Crites, "Storytime," 163.

41. Crites, "Narrative Quality of Experience," 302.

42. Ibid., 302.

43. Gergen and Gergen, "Narratives of the Self," 255.

44. MacIntyre, *After Virtue*, 215–16.

45. Gergen and Gergen, "Social Construction of Narrative Accounts," 175.

46. MacIntyre, *After Virtue*, 215.

47. Gergen and Gergen, "Social Construction of Narrative Accounts," 175.

48. Navone, *Toward a Theology of Story*, 78.

49. Gergen and Gergen, "Narratives of the Self," 256.

50. For more detailed descriptions of social construction theory, see Peter L. Berger and Thomas Luckman, *The Social Construction of Reality* (Garden City, N.Y.: Doubleday & Co., 1966); and K. Gergen, "The Social Constructionist Movement in Modern Psychology," *American Psychologist* 40 (1985): 266–75.

51. Speed, "Reality Exists, OK?" 395.

52. White and Epston, *Narrative Means to Therapeutic Ends*, 4–5.

53. Those not familiar with systems theory could begin by reading E. Mansell Pattison's *Pastor and Parish: A Systems Approach* (Philadelphia: Fortress Press, 1977).

54. Gergen and Gergen, "Social Construction of Narrative Accounts," 174.

55. Sallie TeSelle [McFague], "The Experience of Coming to Belief," *Theology Today* 32, no. 2 (July 1975): 160.

56. James E. Loder, *The Transforming Moment: Understanding Convictional Experiences* (San Francisco: Harper & Row, 1981).

57. Stroup, *Promise of Narrative Theology*, 258.

58. Hauerwas, "Story and Theology," 347.

59. TeSelle [McFague], "Experience of Coming to Belief," 159–60.

60. For careful studies of pastoral care in context, see Larry Kent Graham, *Care of Persons, Care of Worlds: A Psychosystems Approach to Pastoral Care and Counseling* (Nashville: Abingdon Press, 1992), and Maxine Glaz and Jeanne Stevenson Moesnner, *Women in Travail and Transition: A New Pastoral Care* (Minneapolis: Fortress Press, 1991).

Chapter 3. Future Stories
and Human Brokenness

1. See Howard W. Stone, *Crisis Counseling* (Minneapolis: Fortress Press, 1993); David K. Switzer, *The Minister as Crisis Counselor* (Nashville: Abingdon Press, 1986); and Charles V. Gerkin, *Crisis Experience in Modern Life: Theory and Theology for Pastoral Care* (Nashville: Abingdon Press, 1979).

2. Rollo May, *The Meaning of Anxiety*, rev. ed. (New York: W. W. Norton & Co., 1977), 205. May summed up his research on theories of anxiety with this definition: "Anxiety is the apprehension cued off by a threat to some value that the individual holds essential to [her or] his existence as a personality."

3. *Diagnostic and Statistical Manual of Mental Disorders*, 4th ed. (Washington, D.C.: American Psychiatric Association), 764.

4. Ibid., 393.

5. Yalom, *Existential Psychotherapy* (New York: Basic Books, 1980), 8.

6. Gerkin, *Living Human Document*, 33. Italics mine.

7. Charles V. Gerkin, "Crisis Ministry," in *Dictionary of Pastoral Care and Counseling*, ed. Rodney J. Hunter (Nashville: Abingdon Press, 1990), 247–48.

8. Ibid., 247–48.

9. Hauerwas, "Story and Theology," 348.

10. Gerkin, *Living Human Document*, 22.

Chapter 4. Future Stories and Hope

1. Erik H. Erikson, *Insight and Responsibility* (New York: W. W. Norton & Co., 1964), 115.

2. M. Douglas Meeks, *Origins of the Theology of Hope* (Philadelphia: Fortress Press, 1974), 17.

3. Viktor E. Frankl, *Man's Search for Meaning: An Introduction to Logotherapy* (New York: Simon & Schuster, 1984).

4. Viktor E. Frankl, *Psychotherapy and Existentialism* (New York: Washington Square Press, 1967), 5–14.

5. Yalom, *Existential Psychotherapy*, 445.

6. Gabriel Marcel, *Homo Viator: Introduction to a Metaphysic of Hope*, trans. Emma Crauford (New York: Harper & Row, 1962), 11.

7. Ibid., 10.

8. Macquarrie, *In Search of Humanity*, 243.

9. Woodyard, *Beyond Cynicism*, 34.

10. William F. Lynch, *Images of Hope: Imagination as Healer of the Hopeless* (Baltimore: Helicon Press, 1965), 24.

11. Karl Menninger, "Hope," *Pastoral Psychology* 11 (April 1960): 15.

12. Crites, "Storytime," 167.

13. Ezra Stotland, *The Psychology of Hope: An Integration of Experimental, Clinical, and Social Approaches* (San Francisco: Jossey-Bass, 1969), 2.

14. Ibid., 5.

15. Marcel, *Homo Viator*, 32, 45–47.

16. Macquarrie, *In Search of Humanity*, 247.

17. Erikson, *Insight and Responsibility*, 116.

18. Ibid., 117.

19. Jürgen Moltmann, *The Experiment Hope*, ed. and trans. M. Douglas Meeks (Philadelphia: Fortress Press, 1975), 30–43.

20. See ibid., 15–29, and Bloch, *Principle of Hope*, 3: 1183–1353.

21. John Macquarrie, *Principles of Christian Theology*, 2d ed. (New York: Charles Scribner's Sons, 1977), 347–48.

22. See Marcel, *Homo Viator*, 49.

23. Erikson, *Insight and Responsibility*, 117.

24. Dietrich Ritschl, *Memory and Hope: An Inquiry Concerning the Presence of Christ* (New York: Macmillan Co., 1967), 162.

25. Roy W. Fairchild, *Finding Hope Again: A Pastor's Guide to Counseling Depressed Persons* (San Francisco: Harper & Row, 1981), 50–58.

26. Kurt Lewin, *Field Theory in Social Science, Selected Papers*, ed. Dorwin Cartwright (New York: Harper & Brothers, 1951), 53.

27. Ibid., 29.

28. David K. Switzer, *The Dynamics of Grief: Its Source, Pain, and Healing* (Nashville: Abingdon Press, 1970), 205.

29. Navone, *Toward a Theology of Story*, 116.

30. *Origins of the Theology of Hope*, 18.

31. Carrigan, "Where Has Hope Gone?" 47, 49.

32. Woodyard, *Beyond Cynicism*, 15.

33. Navone, *Toward a Theology of Story*, 8.

34. Moltmann, *Experiment Hope*, 47–48.

35. Lynch, *Images of Hope*, 18.

Chapter 5. Future Stories and Despair

1. Joan Nowotny, "Despair and the Object of Hope," in Fitzgerald, *The Sources of Hope*, 44, summarizes Marcel's position as expressed in his *Being and Having*.

2. *Diagnostic and Statistical Manual of Mental Disorders*, 4th ed. (Washington, D.C.: American Psychiatric Association, 1994), 320. In the DSM-III depression was discussed under "Affective Disorders," but in the revised edition (DSM-III-R) and in DSM-IV, depression is identified as a "Mood Disorder."

3. Ibid., 320–23.

4. Ibid., 349.

5. Walter Brueggemann, *Hopeful Imagination: Prophetic Voices in Exile* (Philadelphia: Fortress Press, 1986), 32–43. Also see Brueggemann's *Hope within History* (Atlanta: John Knox Press, 1987), 72–91.

6. Translated by Mark C. Taylor in "Kierkegaard as a Theologian of Hope," *Union Seminary Quarterly Review* 28 (spring 1973): 227.

7. Kierkegaard, *Fear and Trembling/The Sickness unto Death*, 168.

8. Ibid., 168–70.

9. Ibid., 170–75.

10. Crites, "Storytime," 171.

11. Ibid.

12. Ibid., 172.

13. Marcel, *Homo Viator,* 37.

14. Quoted in Nowotny, "Despair and the Object of Hope," 46.

15. Gabriel Marcel, "Desire and Hope," in *Existential Phenomenology,* ed. N. Lawrence and D. O'Conner (Englewood Cliffs, N.J.: Prentice-Hall, 1967), 281.

16. Nowotny, "Despair and the Object of Hope," 46–47.

17. Crites, "Storytime," 168.

18. See James E. Loder, *The Transforming Moment: Understanding Convictional Experiences* (San Francisco: Harper & Row, 1981), 79–91, for an interesting discussion of the void.

19. Ibid., 167–73. On pp. 86–87 the author gives an interesting example from his own experience of how the "Holy" comes into the void.

20. MacIntyre, *After Virtue,* 217.

21. Royal J. Synwolt, "Pastoral Counselor: Harbinger of Hope," *Pastoral Psychology* 22 (May 1971): 6.

22. Frankl, *Man's Search for Meaning.*

23. Erikson, *Insight and Responsibility,* 115–16.

24. Paul Tillich, *The Courage to Be* (New Haven, Conn.: Yale University Press, 1952), 56.

25. Translated from Marcel's "Structure de L'esperance" by Nowotny in "Despair and the Object of Hope," 44.

26. Quoted in Nowotny, "Despair and the Object of Hope," 44.

Chapter 6. The Dynamics of
Hope and Despair

1. Lynch, *Images of Hope,* 163, 171.

2. Hauerwas, "Story and Theology," 348.

3. Paul Pruyser, "Phenomenology and Dynamics of Hoping," *Journal for the Scientific Study of Religion* 3, no. 1 (October 1963): 93.

4. Carrigan, "Where Has Hope Gone?" 45.

5. Marcel, *Homo Viator,* 67.

6. Carrigan, "Where Has Hope Gone?" 44.

7. Mary Louise Bringle, *Despair: Sickness or Sin?* (Nashville: Abingdon Press, 1990), 154–57.

8. Hauerwas, "Story and Theology," 348.

9. Lynch, *Images of Hope,* 24.

10. An interpretation of Marcel in Pruyser's "Phenomenology and Dynamics of Hoping," 91. See also Macquarrie, *In Search of Humanity,* 43–44.

11. Lynch, *Images of Hope,* 38.

12. W. W. Meissner, "Notes on the Psychology of Hope," *Journal of Religion and Health* 12, no. 1 (January 1973), Part II: 121.

13. Lynch, *Images of Hope,* 40. Hopelessness "cannot imagine anything that can be done or that is worth doing," says Pruyser in "Phenomenology and Dynamics of Hoping," 93.

14. Lynch, *Images of Hope,* 26.

15. Ibid., 51.
16. Ibid., 27.
17. Ibid.
18. Carrigan, "Where Has Hope Gone?" 49.
19. Lynch, *Images of Hope*, 209.
20. C.F.D. Moule, *The Meaning of Hope: A Biblical Exposition with Concordance* (Philadelphia: Fortress Press, 1963), 19.
21. Macquarrie, *In Search of Humanity*, 233.
22. John Macquarrie, *Christian Hope* (New York: Seabury Press, 1978), 18.
23. Sartre, *Being and Nothingness*, 539.
24. Navone, *Toward a Theology of Story*, 118.
25. Beavers and Kaslow, "Anatomy of Hope," 125.
26. Nowotny, "Despair and the Object of Hope," 64.
27. Lynch, *Images of Hope*, 19.
28. Carrigan, "Where Has Hope Gone?" 49.
29. Marcel, quoted and translated by Nowotny in "Despair and the Object of Hope," 47.
30. Lynch, *Images of Hope*, 219.
31. Marcel, "Structure de L'esperance," quoted and translated by Nowotny in "Despair and the Object of Hope," 47.
32. Lynch, *Images of Hope*, 136–37.
33. Erikson, *Insight and Responsibility*, 116–17.
34. Beavers and Kaslow, "Anatomy of Hope," 119.
35. Nowotny, "Despair and the Object of Hope," 66.
36. Ibid.
37. Marcel, *Homo Viator*, 10.
38. Schubert Ogden, "The Meaning of Christian Hope," *Union Seminary Quarterly Review* 30 (winter-summer 1975): 159.
39. Marcel, as related by Nowotny in "Despair and the Object of Hope," 57.
40. See Karl Menninger, "Hope," *Pastoral Psychology* 11 (April 1960).
41. Synwolt, "Pastoral Counselor," 11.

Chapter 7. Hearing the Future Story

1. See the essays in George A. Miller and Elizabeth Lenneberg, eds., *Psychology and Biology of Language and Thought* (New York: Academic Press, 1978). For a readable overview, see Harlene Anderson and Harold A. Goolishian, "Human Systems as Linguistic Systems: Preliminary and Evolving Ideas about the Implications for Clinical Theory," *Family Process* 27, no. 4 (December 1988): 371–93.
2. Anderson and Goolishian, "Human Systems," 377.
3. See Paul Watzlawick, *The Language of Change: Elements of Therapeutic Communication* (New York: Basic Books, 1978).
4. Hans-Georg Gadamer, *Truth and Method* (New York: Seabury Press, 1975), 397–447.
5. Anderson and Goolishian, "Human Systems," 380.
6. Ibid., 381.

7. White and Epston, *Narrative Means to Therapeutic Ends*, 17.

8. Gerkin, *Living Human Document*, 26.

9. LeRoy Aden, "Phenomenological Method in Pastoral Care," in the *Dictionary of Pastoral Care and Counseling*, ed. Rodney J. Hunter (Nashville: Abingdon Press, 1990), 911.

10. See Boisen, *Exploration of the Inner World*.

11. William Barrett, *Irrational Man: A Study in Existential Philosophy* (Garden City, N.Y.: Doubleday & Co., 1958), 191.

12. Ben Furman and Tapani Ahola, *Solution Talk: Hosting Therapeutic Conversations* (New York: W. W. Norton & Co., 1992), 106.

13. See Joseph E. Shorr, Gail E. Sobel, Pennee Robin, and Jack A. Connella, *Imagery: Its Many Dimensions and Applications* (New York: Plenum Press, 1980).

14. Crites, "Storytime," 170.

15. Bloch, *Principle of Hope*, 1: 77–113. This section also offers an interesting critique of psychoanalytic focus on night dreams to the exclusion of daydreams.

Chapter 8. Resistance to Exploring Future Stories

1. Richard Driscoll, *Pragmatic Psychotherapy* (New York: Van Nostrand Reinhold Co., 1984), 185.

2. W. Robert Beavers, *Psychotherapy and Growth* (New York: Brunner/Mazel, 1977), 339–41.

Chapter 9. Confronting Dysfunctional Future Stories

1. Gergen and Gergen, "Social Construction of Narrative Accounts," 175–76.

2. For a discussion of various theories, see James A. Hyde, "Story Theology and Family Systems Theory: Contributions to Pastoral Counseling with Families," doctoral dissertation, Southern Baptist Theological Seminary, Louisville, Kentucky, 1988.

3. See Moltmann, *Theology of Hope*.

4. Paul Watzlawick, John H. Weakland, and Richard Fisch, *Change: Principles of Problem Formation and Problem Resolution* (New York: W. W. Norton & Co., 1974).

5. Crites, "Narrative Quality of Experience," 307.

6. Robert Steele, "Deconstructing Histories: Toward a Systematic Criticism of Psychological Narratives," in Sarbin, *Narrative Psychology*, 260.

7. Steve de Shazer, *Clues: Investigating Solutions in Brief Therapy* (New York: W. W. Norton & Co., 1988), 102.

8. Steve de Shazer, *Putting Differences to Work* (New York: W. W. Norton & Co., 1991), 68.

9. Steele, "Deconstructing Histories," 259–73.

10. For a discussion of the relationship between wishing and hoping, see Marcel, *Homo Viator*, 29–67.

Chapter 10. Construction of Hopeful
Future Stories

1. Jürgen Moltmann, foreword to *The Origins of the Theology of Hope*, by M. Douglas Meeks (Philadelphia: Fortress Press, 1974), x.

2. Gerkin, *Living Human Document*, 22.

3. Hauerwas, "Story and Theology," 348.

4. Richard Bandler and John Grinder, *Reframing: Neuro-Linguistic Programming and the Transformation of Meaning*, ed. Steve Andreas and Connirae Andreas (Moab, Utah: Real People Press, 1982).

5. For a summary, see Donald Capps, *Reframing: A New Method in Pastoral Care* (Minneapolis: Fortress Press, 1990).

6. Watzlawick, Weakland, and Fisch, *Change*, 95.

7. See Gerkin, *Living Human Document*, 45–48, for a description of the clashing of horizons, which he takes from Gadamer.

8. Gergen and Gergen, "Social Construction of Narrative Accounts," in Gergen and Gergen, *Historical Social Psychology*, 174–75.

9. Ibid., 178.

10. Richard A. Gardner, *Psychotherapy with Children of Divorce* (New York: Jason Aronson, 1976), 58–59.

11. Some creative techniques can also be gleaned from Ira Progoff in *The Dynamics of Hope: Perspectives of Process in Anxiety and Creativity, Imagery and Dreams* (New York: Dialogue House Library, 1985).

12. William H. O'Hanlon and Michele Weiner-Davis, *In Search of Solutions: A New Direction in Psychotherapy* (New York: W. W. Norton & Co., 1989), 106. Also see de Shazer, *Clues*, 51.

13. O'Hanlon and Weiner-Davis, *In Search of Solutions*, 106–10.

14. Furman and Ahola, *Solution Talk*, 91–106.

15. See de Shazer, *Putting Differences to Work*.

16. Furman and Ahola, *Solution Talk*, 102–3.

17. O'Hanlon and Weiner-Davis, *In Search of Solutions*, 154–58.

Index of Scripture,
Names, and Subjects

Printed in the United States
55753LVS00007B/274-291

9 780664 255886